Images for Eternity

Egyptian Art from Berkeley and Brooklyn

by Richard Fazzini

The Fine Arts Museums of San Francisco

and The Brooklyn Museum

1975

Published for the exhibition at the
M. H. de Young Memorial Museum
July 26—October 18 1975.
With loans from The Brooklyn Museum
and the Robert H. Lowie Museum of
Anthropology, University of California,
Berkeley.

Preface by Ian McKibbin White
Designed by Ronald Gordon
Edited by Elizabeth Riefstahl and
Eleanor F. Wedge

ISBN 0-913696-26-9 (Hard Cover)
ISBN 0-913696-27-7 (Paper Cover)
Library of Congress Catalog Card
number 75-13976

Frontispiece: Cat. 41, detail of the statue
of Senwosret-senebefny.

Printed by the Rapoport Printing
Corporation.

Produced by the Publishing Center for
Cultural Resources, New York.
Manufactured in the United States
of America.

Contents

Chronology

(only kings mentioned in the book are listed)

Predynastic Period
(pre-4000–3100/2950 B.C.)

Early Dynastic Period
(3100/2950–2635 B.C.)
Dynasty I
King Djet
Dynasty II
King Khasekhem
King Khasekhemuwy

Old Kingdom
Dynasty III (2635–2570 B.C.)
King Djoser
Dynasty IV (2570–2450 B.C.)
King Sneferu
King Cheops
King Radedef
King Chephren
King Mycerinus
Dynasty V (2450–2290 B.C.)
King Nyuserre
Dynasty VI (2290–2155 B.C.)
King Pepy I
King Pepy II
Dynasties VII and VIII
(2155–2135 B.C.)

First Intermediate Period
Dynasties IX and X
(2134–2040 B.C.)
Dynasty XI—first part
(2134–2040 B.C.)
King Mentuhotep II

Middle Kingdom
Dynasty XI—second part
(2040–1991 B.C.)
King Mentuhotep II
King Mentuhotep III
King Mentuhotep IV
Dynasty XII (1991–1785 B.C.)
King Amenemhat I
King Sesostris I
King Amenemhat II
King Sesostris II
King Sesostris III
King Amenemhat III
Dynasty XIII—first part
(1785–1715 B.C.)

Second Intermediate Period
Dynasty XIII—second part
(1715–1650 B.C.)
Dynasty XIV (1715–1650 B.C.)
Dynasty XV (1650–1540 B.C.)
Dynasty XVI (1650–1550 B.C.)
Dynasty XVII (1650–1550 B.C.)

The New Kingdom
Dynasty XVIII
(1550–1305 B.C.)
King Ahmose
King Amenhotep I
King Tuthmosis I
Queen Hatshepsut
King Tuthmosis III
King Amenhotep II
King Tuthmosis IV
King Amenhotep III
King Amenhotep IV
  (Akhenaten)
King Tutankhamen
King Aye
King Horemheb
Dynasty XIX (1305–1196 B.C.)
King Sety I
King Ramesses II
King Merenptah
Dynasty XX (1196–1080 B.C.)
King Ramesses III
High Priest of Amun Herihor

Third Intermediate Period
Dynasty XXI (1080–945 B.C.)
Dynasty XXII: Libyan kings
(945–715 B.C.)
King Osorkon II
King Sheshonq III
Dynasty XXIII: Libyan kings
(818–720 B.C.)
King Iuput I
King Iuput II
Dynasty XXIV: Libyan kings
(727–715 B.C.)
Dynasty XXV—first part:
Nubian kings (750–715 B.C.)
King Kashta
King Piankhy

Late Period (750–30 B.C.)
Dynasty XXV—second part:
Nubian kings (715–656 B.C.)
King Shabako
King Taharqa
Dynasty XXVI (664–525 B.C.)
King Psamtik I
King Necho II
King Psamtik III
Dynasty XXVII: Persian
domination (525–404 B.C.)
Dynasty XXVIII (404–399 B.C.)
Dynasty XXIX (399–380 B.C.)
Dynasty XXX (380–342 B.C.)
King Nectanebo I
King Nectanebo II
Dynasty XXXI: Persian
domination (342–332 B.C.)
Macedonian Period
(332–305 B.C.)
Alexander the Great
Ptolemy Lagou
Ptolemaic Period (305–30 B.C.)
King Ptolemy I
King Ptolemy I
Cleopatra VII
Roman conquest of Egypt
in 30 B.C.

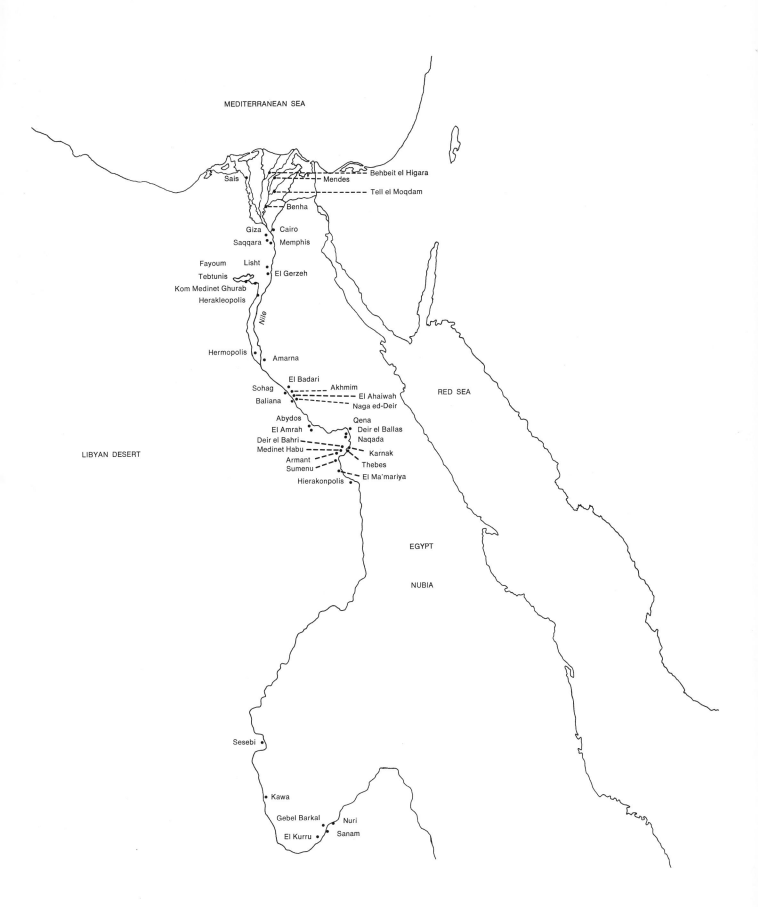

MEDITERRANEAN SEA

Behbeit el Higara

Mendes

Tell el Moqdam

Sais

Benha

Giza   Cairo

Saqqara   Memphis

Fayoum   Lisht

Tebtunis

Kom Medinet Ghurab   El Gerzeh

Herakleopolis

Nile

Hermopolis   Amarna

El Badari

Sohag   Akhmim

El Ahaiwah

Baliana   Naga ed-Deir

Abydos   Qena

El Amrah   Deir el Ballas

Deir el Bahri   Naqada

Medinet Habu   Karnak

Armant   Thebes

Sumenu

Hierakonpolis   El Ma'mariya

LIBYAN DESERT

RED SEA

EGYPT

NUBIA

Sesebi

Kawa

Gebel Barkal   Nuri

El Kurru   Sanam

page vii

Preface

The art of ancient Egypt is seldom seen in San Francisco. Now in this extraordinary exhibition we have a comprehensive survey of the full sweep of Egyptian art from 4000 B.C. to 40 B.C. The last major exhibition here, in 1962, was of the spectacular find from the tomb of Tutankhamen which, however, represented only a brief moment in Egyptian history.

The idea for this rare opportunity was born on April 3, 1971, when my good friend and former associate from The Brooklyn Museum, Bernard V. Bothmer, Curator of Egyptian and Classical Art, was visiting the Robert H. Lowie Museum of Anthropology, Berkeley, California. He was impressed with the wealth of the Old Kingdom and later material that had been given to the University of California between 1901 and 1904 by Phoebe Apperson Hearst.

Knowing of our interest in ancient art, Mr. Bothmer observed that the famous Brooklyn collection of Egyptian art might be stored during a renovation of their galleries beginning in 1975. He asked if it would not be better that a selection of these treasures, enriched by objects from the Lowie Museum holdings, be put on view in San Francisco. We enthusiastically agreed.

Thus we are indebted greatly to Mr. Bothmer and to Professor William Russell Bascom, Director of the Robert H. Lowie Museum of Anthropology, whose generosity made this exhibition possible. We are grateful also to Richard Fazzini, Associate Curator in Brooklyn's Department of Egyptian and Classical Art, who has been responsible for the selection of objects and the text of this useful catalogue, and to Frank Norick, Principal Museum Anthropologist, whose assistance on the Lowie Museum segment of the exhibition was invaluable.

The organization of the exhibition at The Fine Arts Museums of San Francisco was the responsibility of F. Lanier Graham, Chief Curator, Jane Gray Nelson, Assistant Curator in charge of Ancient Art, and Thomas H. Garver, Curator in Charge of Exhibitions. The installation was designed by Royal Basich; construction by the staff under the supervision of Raymond Raczkowski, Principal Preparator. The exhibition is sponsored by the Museum Society of The Fine Arts Museums of San Francisco.

Ian McKibbin White
Director of Museums
The Fine Arts Museums
of San Francisco

Foreword

This book was written to provide the visitor to the Exhibition with a visual record of the objects encountered as well as to provide the reader with background material about ancient Egypt and its art which the author believes will enhance the understanding and enjoyment of the objects included in the Exhibition.

The entries for most of the objects are deliberately brief so that the visitor may read them quickly and devote more time looking at the objects themselves. Inasmuch as this catalogue was not written for specialists, the text of some of the entries is as much or more concerned with general aspects of the art and culture also relevant to other pieces than with specific data about each object. However, the interested reader will find details of provenance, measurements, and a selective bibliography for each object in Concordance I. In Chapters I through V the objects, as well as some of the points raised about them in the entries, are discussed in connection with the history, culture, and art of ancient Egypt during five major chronological periods. The Introduction is devoted primarily to a commentary on certain more general aspects of Egyptian art and culture.

Objects from the Robert H. Lowie Museum of Anthropology with numbers prefixed 6 are from excavations sponsored by Mrs. Phoebe Apperson Hearst. Cat. 42, 56, and 95 were purchased and donated to the Museum by Mrs. Hearst.

With the exception of the following pieces, all Brooklyn Museum objects were purchased from the Charles Edwin Wilbour Memorial Fund. Cat. 1: Brooklyn Museum Excavations. Cat. 63: Charles Edwin Wilbour Collection. Cat. 64 and 76: gifts of The Egypt Exploration Society. Cat. 77: Museum Collection Fund. Cat. 100: Gift of A. T. White and G. T. Brackett.

Considerations of space prevent the author from acknowledging by name all those who have assisted him in the preparation of this catalogue as well as with other matters pertaining to the Exhibition. This is particularly true of the members of the staff of the Department of Egyptian and Classical Art, The Brooklyn Museum, all of whom have helped in ways too numerous to mention. To Mr. William Lyle, The Brooklyn Museum's photographer, belongs the credit for the photographs for the frontispiece as well as for catalogue entries 1, 11, 18, 20a, 58, 64-65, 74-75, 79-80, 84-85, 87-88, 91, 93, 104a, 105-107, and 110.

The author also wishes to acknowledge the assistance and cooperation of Mr. Ian McKibbin White, Director of Museums, The Fine Arts Museums of San Francisco, and the following members of his staff: F. Lanier Graham, Thomas H. Garver, and Jane Gray Nelson. He is also indebted to Mr.

William Russell Bascom, Director of the Robert H. Lowie Museum of Anthropology, and Mr. Frank Norick, Principal Museum Anthropologist, for their assistance with matters pertaining to objects from the Robert H. Lowie Museum of Anthropology in the Exhibition. The photographs of those objects illustrated were produced by the Robert H. Lowie Museum of Anthropology and The Fine Arts Museums of San Francisco.

As it was impossible to include bibliographical references not specifically related to objects in the Exhibition, a great many individuals responsible for most of the facts and ideas contained in this book, whose names would otherwise appear in footnotes, must remain anonymous to all but themselves and their colleagues.

The author further wishes to express his gratitude to Francis F. Dobo and M. J. Gladstone of the Publishing Center for Cultural Resources for their work in arranging for the production of the catalogue and to Ronald Gordon for its design.

Finally, the author wishes to thank four special people for their help in the production of his manuscript. The first three are Eleanor Wedge, Elizabeth Riefstahl, and Lillian Flowerman. The fourth is the author's wife, Barbara Giella, to whom he is also indebted for her sacrifices and moral support during the months when the manuscript was written.

Richard Fazzini
The Brooklyn Museum

Introduction

Art does not exist in a vacuum. It expresses the circumstances of its makers. It is created to serve the needs generated by their feelings, beliefs and aspirations.

The ancient Egyptians were an essentially religious people who perceived their universe as populated by supernatural and divine powers. A main task of the state religion was the establishment of a mutually beneficial relationship between the people and these powers. In a more limited sphere (and especially in terms of his eternal survival) this was the task of the individual.

Under such circumstances it is no wonder that much Egyptian art was created as a luxurious tool to serve urgent religious and magical purposes. It is also not surprising that the art generally was not individualistic but instead conformed to certain norms determined by commonly shared beliefs. That the art maintained certain of those forms over the course of three millennia testifies to the enduring nature of those beliefs.

Any introduction to the art of ancient Egypt must therefore be prefaced by a sketch of the country's religion. In turn, at the risk of overemphasizing the influence of Egypt's climate and geography upon those beliefs, such a sketch must begin with a brief description of Egypt itself.

Geographically, ancient Egypt was divided into two separate zones. In the North was the Delta with its broad, flat expanses of alluvial plains and swamps. In the South were the narrow bands of cultivable land, deposited over the millennia by the annual flooding of the Nile, flanking the river and hemmed in by the cliffs of the surrounding desert. Politically also the land was divided in two, although the boundaries of these parts did not precisely coincide with the juncture of the Delta and the Nile Valley. From the time of the first political unification of the country the pharaoh was not "King of Egypt" but "King of Upper and Lower Egypt" (Fig. 1). Taking their orientation from the Nile, which flows from South to North, for the Egyptians southern Egypt was Upper Egypt and northern Egypt was Lower Egypt.

The physical distinctions between North and South were undoubtedly important to the creation of art, and in some ways their effects are obvious. Thus, with no desert cliffs, the Delta lacks the decorated rock-cut tombs found throughout the length of the Nile Valley to the south. Furthermore, with the quarries mainly situated at great distances from the Delta, more use seems to have been made of mud brick in the construction of temples

Fig. 1. King Sety I seated between the goddesses of Upper and Lower Egypt. The gods Horus and Thoth are depicted as binding together the heraldic plants of the Two Lands. Drawing of a relief in the temple of Sety I at Abydos. Dynasty XIX.

and tombs in the North than in the South. The less obvious effects the northern terrain might have had upon the arts cannot yet be precisely defined or measured. However it seems that the broader expanses of the Delta, open to foreign influences from both the East and West, may have made the area more amenable to local cultural variations than was generally true of the more funnel-like Southlands. Enough is known about the Delta to make it clear that—with the exceptions of the appearance of non-Egyptian culture as, for example, during the Second Intermediate Period—after the first cultural blending between North and South and their initial political unification, the cultural and artistic differences between the two regions were generally no greater than variations on a single theme. In fact, those aspects of the ancient Egyptians' environment which seem to be most clearly reflected in their attitudes and beliefs were common to both parts of the land.

In our times, especially in the West, it is impossible for us to comprehend the impact of an environment upon a people most of whom were tied to their locality, most of whom were farmers dependent upon and working in harmony with the forces of nature, forces as yet unexplained.

The most striking characteristic of the ancient Egyptian environment is its predictability. The landscape might differ dramatically between North and South, but within each region the terrain displays a remarkable degree of regularity. Throughout the country the great natural phenomena—the daily course of the sun through a heaven only infrequently obscured by clouds and the annual flooding of the Nile, saving the land from the withering heat and dryness of summer—assumed awe–inspiring prominence.

These forces of nature, their regular rhythms and the uniformity of the landscape must have been major factors in the formulation of the ancient Egyptians' conception of their universe as functioning according to unvarying patterns. Indeed, these forces were perceived as divine beings whose modes of action were established on "The First Occasion": the creation of the universe.

Versions of the creation were current in the myths of ancient Egypt. However, a general theme was that the creation entailed the bringing of life, shape, and order to a part of a limitless, dark, and undifferentiated primeval watery chaos of nonexistence—in the manner in which small islands of land teeming with life would arise each year from the receding flood waters of the Nile. First a creator god came into being. He in turn brought into being other gods who, although distinct entities, remained manifestations of the creator himself. The gods, however were not all the things that were brought into being on this "First Occasion." The entire universe was created, including a world in which man might live, as well as religion, law, and kingship. In other words all the elements required for a stable society came into existence at this time. Outside the created universe chaos still existed, but inside the universe everything was perfect and adhered to a god–given scheme of things. This divine order was personified in a goddess named Maat, whose name is often translated as "truth" or "justice". These, however, are only two of her aspects, for she embodies the harmonious coexistence and interaction of all the elements of the universe which must function in their proper manner to prevent the universe from distintegrating back into chaos. Maat thus governed the great natural cycles of the sun, the Nile, the seasons, and the stars. However, as man was a part of the universe, Maat also governed his way of life, his relations with the gods and with his fellows.

Living in such an environment and holding such beliefs, it is not surprising that the Egyptians had a periodic sense of time linked to the cycles of nature which they perceived as part of a divine order continuously repeated. Nor should it be surprising, inasmuch as the universe was created whole and perfect at the beginning, that the past should constitute a valid model for the present. Sometimes recourse to the past was had for specific purposes. For example, a king of Dynasty XIII wishing to have a new statue made for the god Osiris at Abydos, commanded a search of old temple archives to determine the original divinely ordained appearance of the god's statue so that the new work might be based on that model. It is therefore not difficult to understand how, on many occasions, the arts might display strong archaizing tendencies without their being a mere empty copying of the past. Such tendencies were most prominent during or just after times of internal disturbance when the feeling that the country had strayed from its correct and ideal state would be most strongly felt. Indeed, age brought sanctity to things, especially those of a religious nature. For example, one of the magic spells of benefit to the deceased contained in the collections of such spells now called "The Book of the Dead" was, according to tradition, first discovered as an inscription on an object of great antiquity hidden in a temple. It is clear that the spell's value was somehow enhanced by its great age.

The beliefs of the Egyptians therefore bespeak a resiliency against sudden or dramatic change partly induced by their physical environment. However, these beliefs were also dependent upon, and in turn would have influenced, other aspects of Egyptian history and society. After a possible strong outside influence on the initial development of Egyptian civilization, Egypt's relative isolation from the rest of the ancient world until the country's domination by kings of foreign ancestry in the Second Intermediate Period also helped maintain the status quo. The fact that life expectancy was in general low, combined with conservative methods of education, also mitigated against change. As an adolescent, the average ancient Egyptian had to shoulder adult responsibilities. For the masses of peasants, their circumscribed lives on the land would, in general, have differed little from year to year or even from generation to generation. For the well to do and especially for royalty, there was little incentive for change. Life for them was comfortable, and because of the religious nature of the Egyptian state and the role played by the kings, was apt to remain so. While the belief in a divine order may have predated the unification of Egypt under a single ruler, it is clear that throughout Egyptian history Maat was identified with a hierarchical Egyptian state governed by a king in whose hands all power theoretically resided. Indeed, it had been the emergence of a strong kingship which had first brought order and unity to the land, making possible large—scale utilization of Egypt's rich natural resources. That the kingship was the cornerstone of the Egyptian state and Egypt's prosperity may be seen by the fact that during those periods when the kingship was weak the land became politically fragmented, civil warfare erupted, Egypt fell prey to incursions by foreigners, the prosperity of the land diminished, and the quality of art declined.

The great cycles of nature, so pervasive in Egypt, may in part have accounted for the Egyptians' perception of the universe as functioning according to a continuous repetition of a divine pattern. This pattern, like those natural cycles, was a sequence of birth, death, and rebirth; however, rebirth following death was not inevitable. The Nile, for example, did not bring the proper flood level each and every year. Sometimes it brought too little water and the crops would not grow, while sometimes it brought too much, resulting in destruction as well as famine. And even when the flood reached an optimum level, cooperative effort on a large scale was needed to make it advantageous to the land. So too did the divine order need constant tending. Just as the creation of the Egyptian state had not brought its order to the entire world, so too the creation of the universe had not eliminated chaos. It had only imposed form and order upon a small portion of it. Outside the area of order dark forces still threatened. Only the continued proper functioning of each part of the complex mechanism of the universe, in both the divine and earthly spheres as well as in the relations between the two, could protect the existence of the ideal scheme of things. No small part of this task was assigned by the gods to the Egyptian kings. This responsibility commanded the support of his people since Egypt's well—being depended in both theory and actuality upon its proper execution. The pharaoh's direct responsibility to the gods was to provide them with that which they required and desired; and according to Egyptian theology, divine needs and demands were similar to those of human beings, both living and dead.

The kings of Egypt furnished their gods with houses: the famous temples of Egypt. These structures, like most tombs, were generally made of stone rather than of the less durable materials used even for royal earthly dwell-

Fig. 2. Stela with a representation of a falcon atop a palace within which is a serpent: the writing of the Horus name of King Djet (Serpent). From Abydos. Dynasty I. Paris, Musée du Louvre.

ings, because they were built for eternity. Temples were those places where the deities consented to dwell, where their divine essences deigned to become manifest in the cult images provided for that purpose. However, temples were not houses of god in the modern sense, as they were not places of congregational worship. On the contrary, they were "castles of the gods" in which the deities lived as lords attended by their servants, the priests. The people might be admitted to the outermost areas, corresponding to the more public rooms of a residence. In the rear part of the temple, however, only certain priestly personnel might enter; and it was here that the most essential part of the cult was conducted: the daily ablutions of, and offerings to the cult statue of the temple's deity. These offerings consisted to a great extent of food; and after the deity was magically satisfied with his meals the same offerings were presented to the statues of those important persons who had been granted the privilege of having their sculptures placed in the temple so that their spirits might magically partake of the god's bounty. Thus, the statues of Yii (Cat. 71) and Pedimahes (Cat. 94) bear inscriptions invoking their participation in the food offerings presented to the gods. Indeed, the inscriptions on the latter work invoke for its owner the "offerings which are in Upper Egypt and the provisions which are in Lower Egypt." Finally, such offerings were divided among the temple personnel.

While in practice it was the priests who, as delegates of the king, conducted the services for the gods, in theory it was the king himself who performed these rituals each day in each temple. This reflects the fact that, just as the king commanded the construction of the temples, it was the royal endowments that maintained the cults. Moreover, it was the pharaoh who was in theory the only being entitled to and qualified for divine service, as he in a way was one of the gods.

It was believed that after death the Egyptian king was transformed into a god and therefore was provided with a funerary temple where his cult might be practiced, in addition to a permanent earthly dwelling in the form of a tomb. Inasmuch as blessings might flow from the king in death as in life—with those buried near him sharing in the offerings made to the dead king—his relatives and courtiers often built their tombs in the immediate vicinity of that of their ruler.

The exact nature of the living king, however, is a much discussed problem. Earlier scholars generally agreed that the king was believed to be a living god. He is called a god in the inscriptions and identified with various deities, including Horus, while the deceased king is identified as his father Osiris, god of the dead. However, recent investigations of the Egyptian kingship have stressed the fact that the king had a mortal nature. Although the office of kingship was divine and the individual king an embodiment of that office, each ruler had a simultaneously human aspect. The emphasis given to these two aspects or roles of the king varied from period to period depending upon changes in Egyptian society. For example, in the earliest historical period the divine aspect of the king, the king as Horus (Fig. 2), was stressed, and this continued to be true into Dynasty IV of the Old Kingdom (Fig. 3). However, already in that Dynasty there was a shift in emphasis from the king as god to the king as son of god, more specifically the son of Re the sun god. And with this change, in Dynasties V and VI

Fig. 3. Statue of King Chephren with Horus as a falcon perched behind his head. From the King's funerary temple at Giza. Dynasty IV. Cairo, Egyptian Museum.

greater stress came to be placed on the human and personal aspect of the king. That such a change in emphasis should have accompanied an apparent decline in royal power is no more surprising than the fact that in the New Kingdom several kings, most notably Amenhotep III, Akhenaten, and Ramesses II, faced with forces eroding their power, should have stressed their own divinity as a countermeasure to those forces.

These changes in the stress placed on the role of the king had, as will be discussed in the following chapters, great effects on the nature of the art produced; but, as we have already noted, there were also strong forces conducive to continuity.

The identification of each living king with the god Horus and each dead king with his father Osiris would alone indicate that the kingship was conceived as a cycle; there is abundant other evidence to confirm this view. In fact, each king's reign was but one link in a chain of kingship and marked another repetition of the divine cycle of the universe. Even if the personal and human aspect of king emerges to some extent, the actual events of each reign are subordinate to the cyclical return of events because each reign must, in theory, be like the others. Each king accomplishes Maat anew. His accession becomes a repetition of the creation, and his death the end of a cycle which brings a new beginning in the person of his successor. The king performs a history that has already been written. In a way he plays the role of the creator god; and, inasmuch as what he is to create is to be created according to a preordained pattern, the typical takes precedence over the specific and the individual is also subsumed into the typical. That is, for example, the king may actually defeat Egypt's enemies in battle; however, that event is more often commemorated in a symbolic pose of triumph, such as that seen in Cat. 36b, rather than in a detailed and individualized rendering of the actual event (Fig. 4). Moreover, even if the king had never led an army into battle, he may be so represented, because part of the divine plan is that Egypt's enemies be crushed, that they be under the feet of pharaoh (Fig. 5 and Cat. 40). Just as Egypt might be identified with the ordered universe, so her enemies might be the embodiment of the forces of chaos which need to be held in check. When Egypt's enemies are not

Fig. 4. The Battle of Kadesh. Drawing of a relief depicting one of King Ramesses II's military operations in Syria. The original is on the gateway of a temple at Thebes. Dynasty XIX.

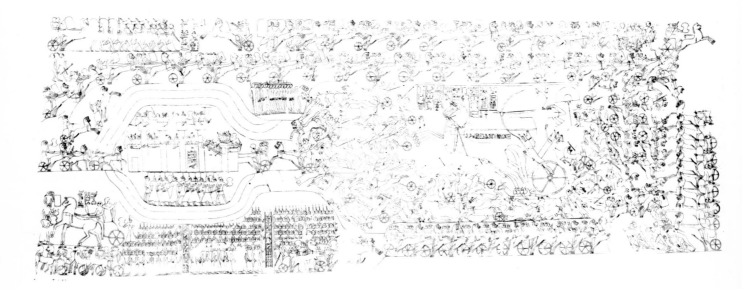

neatly symbolized as defeated (Cat. 36b and Cat. 40a), they are shown in chaotic disarray before the majesty of pharaoh (Fig. 5 and 4).

Scenes of the king defeating Egypt's enemies normally adorned the more public parts of temples. Such scenes often flanked doorways and, from the New Kingdom onward, they were a favorite motif for the decoration of the large temple gateways called pylons (Fig. 6). There they might commemorate a personal achievement of the king, serve as propaganda for his military policy, and display his superhuman strength and authority. However, inasmuch as it was believed that representations and inscriptions might be magically animated to become actually what they said and depicted, such representations are more than symbols; they were believed to ward off evil from the temples and their divine residents.

These beliefs clearly resulted in a high degree of iconographical, although not stylistic, uniformity and continuity in the art created for the temples. Although variations exist in the mythology and cult practices associated with each deity (and these also changed with time), certain basic elements of the cult ritual did not vary dramatically from deity to deity. Neither did the blessings the king received from the gods in return for his efforts on their behalf, the blessings of eternal life, prosperity, health, stability, joy, and dominion. If what was represented in the art might magically become real then the art would render the religious truths and its subject matter would change only when that truth also changed.

Inasmuch as all offerings in the temple were generally made by the king only he is represented as making offerings to the gods (Cat. 66, 77, 106, and 107) just as it is he who primarily is shown receiving blessings from them

Fig. 5. Statue of King Khasekhem. The base is decorated with representations of the King's defeated enemies. From Hierakonpolis. Dynasty II. Oxford, Ashmolean Museum.

Fig. 6. Reconstruction of a model of a temple gateway. The original model was created for King Sety I. It was found at Tell el Yahudiya. Dynasty XIX. Brooklyn, The Brooklyn Museum.

in return (Cat. 34, 35, 62, and 66). In general, as in the reliefs on a model of
a temple entrance showing King Sety I making offerings (Fig. 6), the king
faces in toward the gods. To be sure the gods are not represented here
but only named in the inscriptions. When gods were represented they face
outward from the house they inhabited. Thus temple reliefs set up a
motion along the temple's axis toward the sanctuary in the rear. There
are, however, exceptions to this rule. On gateways where the king is
depicted defeating his enemies or hunting wild animals—both the embodi-
ments of the powers of chaos—he may be shown facing outward from the
doorway, for he is driving those forces from the temple.

Elements of temple decoration also take their orientation from the
points of the compass. For example, in representations of the king which
flank doorways it was common practice for the figure on the south side
of the portal to be shown wearing the crown of Upper Egypt and the figure
on the north side that of Lower Egypt.

The iconography of royal temple statuary also reflects the royal functions. Statues of the king seated or striding placed in the temple made the
king's presence there magically permanent. Colossal sculptures of this
type, especially when placed before the temple gateway clearly demonstrate the king's piety and power (Fig. 6), while kneeling and prostrate
figures of the king presenting offerings also served to perpetuate the king's
ritual role in the temple. Small figures of this type (Cat. 98), sometimes
part of cult objects used by priests, might also serve to make the king
present during the actual performance of the ritual.

Cult apparatuses in temples were often elaborate, and this was especially
true of one sort, the boats of the gods. These vessels, as may be seen in an
ornate tomb painting of Dynasty XX (Fig. 7), were made of various materials and decorated with figures, often in bronze, of the king, sphinxes (Cat.
78), and various deities. Such boats were used to carry the images of the
gods in religious processions.

Large-scale statues of deities were also fashioned (Cat. 56) for temples
as were group sculptures of the king with the gods; but these should not
be confused with the cult images, generally small, which were the main
focus of the temple ritual. The latter were often made of precious materials such as gold, and very few have been preserved.

Among the most common temple sculptures are figures of lions (Cat. 11)
and sphinxes (Fig. 6 and Cat. 39) to guard the sacred precincts—cemeteries
as well as temples. The exact meaning of the sphinx, a creature with a
human head and a lion's body, is still uncertain. In general, the member of
royalty so depicted is the king. However, as Cat. 39 demonstrates, queens
could also be so shown.

The status of Egyptian queens, all of whom were married to a "god"
(the king) and some of whom were mothers of future "gods" was always
exalted; and, as will be noted in a later chapter, this was especially the case
in the New Kingdom. In general, queens only ruled the country either
when there was no male heir to the throne or when the heir was a minor
(Cat. 19). However, in Dynasty XVIII Hatshepsut served as the main ruler
in a co-regency with Tuthmosis III; and later in the Dynasty Queens Tiye
and Nefertiti, mother and wife of Akhenaten, were represented smiting
Egypt's enemies. Nefertiti was also shown alone, without her husband,

Fig. 7. Drawing of a painting of a sacred boat of the god Amun. The original is in a private tomb at Thebes. Dynasty XX.

offering to the god, thereby constituting one of the general exceptions to the rule that it was the king who was represented officiating in the temples. Later, during Dynasties XXI through XXVI when the power of the god Amun was at its height, royal women bearing the title "Divine Consort of Amun," who were "married" to that deity, exercised one of the most important religious and political offices in the land and consequently figured prominently in the art of the time.

In fact, the general status of women was quite high in ancient Egypt; and it appears that they enjoyed equal legal rights with men, being able, for example, to own and dispose of their own property, work outside the home, and serve the deities as priestesses. However, this does not mean that Egyptian society was egalitarian in the full and modern sense of that term. Men took precedence over women professionally, and lives of wealthy women, as is indicated by the most common feminine title, "Mistress of the House," were generally limited to home and family. This is clearly the impression given in funerary reliefs and paintings where it is the husband who is represented in official capacities and where, even in domestic scenes, he takes precedence over the wife. The husband is the more active of the two and sometimes is drawn on an unnaturally larger scale. Women of those social classes which could afford to build tombs sometimes had tombs of their own. But most tombs belong to men whose wives were buried with them. One male attitude toward women and their place in society is conveyed in part of "The Teachings of Ptahhotep," a compilation of maxims for success in life attributed to a Vizier of the Old Kingdom. It is advised not to raise one's wife to a position of power but to treat her well, for she is "profitable land for her lord" in return for whose support she gives her body.

Besides temples dedicated to the gods, pharaohs constructed their funerary temples in which the king was a resident deity. Prior to the New Kingdom the royal funerary temples were directly connected to their owners' tombs and were primarily dedicated to the cult services for the deceased king. Accordingly, their decoration differed from that of the gods' temples in that a major motif of the reliefs was the king receiving offerings. These were often shown brought to him by long processions of figures similar to those of Cat. 97b, but inscribed to indicate that they were personifications of the royal estates dedicated to the upkeep of the king's cult. The decoration of such temples also consisted of representations of the king with the gods, although the emphasis was on the king receiving the god's blessings rather than the king presenting offerings. However, the theme of the king performing other duties of his office was not absent from the walls of these edifices. For example, a major motif of the decoration was that of the king defeating Egypt's enemies.

In the New Kingdom the royal funerary temples were constructed separately from the tombs. They had also, with a shift in emphasis of the king's status vis–à–vis the gods, become temples in which the cult rites of

Fig. 8. Vignette from a funerary papyrus depicting the deceased in his tomb. At the entrance of the tomb a priest, followed by the grieving widow, performs a ritual to animate the dead man's mummy. The deceased's Ba is shown flying down the shaft from the entrance of the tomb to the burial chamber below. New Kingdom. Paris, Musée du Louvre.

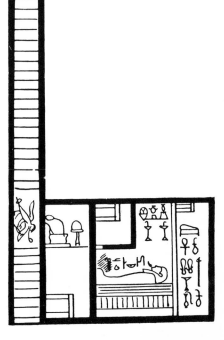

various deities, especialy Amun of Thebes, were conducted and in which a cult for the deceased pharaoh was also celebrated. Their decoration consequently was more similar to that of contemporary temples to the gods than was the decoration of the earlier royal mortuary temples to temples of the gods.

On a less exalted scale those private persons who could afford to do so attempted to secure their own eternal survival in a manner essentially similar to that of the kings.

The funerary beliefs of the ancient Egyptians are not easily explained. For example, just as the Egyptians' conception of the nature of the universe is alien to our own thought, so also there is no ancient Egyptian concept analagous to the modern idea of a human soul. The Egyptians conceived a plurality of modes of existence after death. One of these, the *Ba*, although both spiritual and corporeal, and not divorced from the body of the deceased, perhaps comes closest to our concept of soul. If the proper rituals and offerings were performed, a person's *Ba* could become animated. Pictured in the form of a human-headed bird (Fig. 8 and Cat. 110), it could eat, drink and engage in other activities known in life. It might also come and go from the tomb. During life and death each person also had a *Ka,* a manifestation of his or her vital energy, the receptacle of the forces through which all life flourished.

If the great natural cycles of birth, death, and rebirth were one basis for the Egyptians' belief in an afterlife, another may have been the manner in which a corpse buried under a shallow layer of the warm, dry sands of the desert might be dessicated into a natural mummy. If his body might survive, so might the individual; and inasmuch as the Egyptians do not appear to have made a complete distinction between the spiritual and corporeal elements of the deceased, or to have conceived of a permanent afterlife totally divorced from the body, the dead had need of a body, shelter, and sustenance.

While the great masses of the Egyptian populace might hope for no more than burial in a shallow grave together with a few offerings, wealthier Egyptians sought to preserve their bodies by means of mummification and to protect them by placing them in tombs which served as eternal homes. They furnished these tombs with equipment needed for life, and they arranged for offerings, especially of food and drink, to be made after death. Moreover, in order to ensure magically that what they needed and wanted might be available, these tombs were decorated in a manner to enable the deceased both to survive and to enjoy as full an existence in the hereafter as the religious beliefs of the time permitted.

The earliest of the beliefs concerning the afterlife centered upon life in the tomb and the reanimated body. In later times, as is discussed in the following chapters, private persons came to aspire to an existence outside the tomb in the company of the gods. These and other changes in funerary beliefs had a great effect upon the decoration of tombs and on funerary equipment. For example, in the earlier periods, coffins and sarcophagi were conceived as houses and were often decorated, as were early tombs, with a representation of a facade (such as that in Fig. 2) like that of earthly dwellings. In later periods the dead were buried in anthropoid coffins identifying the deceased with the mummiform god Osiris and protected by representations of various deities (Cat. 102). Similarly, because during the earlier periods the existence within the tomb was held to resemble that on earth, the noble dead came to equip themselves with figures of servants who might replace the servants they had known in life (Cat. 27). The later belief in an existence in the realm of Osiris, where one might be called upon to work, required a different type of servant figure—to act as a substitute for the deceased. These figures (Cat. 92), which first appeared in the Middle Kingdom, were originally called *shawabtis,* a word of uncertain meaning. However, by the New Kingdom they had come to be called *ushabtis,* which means "Ones who answer." These figures were inscribed with texts which magically ensured that they would "answer" in place of the deceased whenever he might be called by the gods to labor for them.

Prior to the time when private persons came to have direct access to the gods, the dead had no need of objects such as canopic jars (Cat. 79). These vessels, in which the internal organs of the deceased were placed, were identified with funerary deities, and by inscription also magically linked the deceased with those deities.

Changes in private funerary beliefs were greater than those in the beliefs concerning the cult of the gods. Therefore the iconography of tomb decoration underwent greater change than that of temple decoration. However, even in tomb decoration there was a remarkable degree of continuity because new ideas did not automatically replace old ideas. Both new and old could and often did coexist as simultaneously valid.

In the earlier periods of Egyptian history, when the postmortem existence was conceived as similar to life on earth the decorations of tombs consisted primarily of representations of the deceased receiving offerings (Cat. 17, 29, 30, and 31) and of scenes of the *type* of life the deceased had led and wished to continue to enjoy for eternity; the king and the gods, if in some way magically ensuring that existence, were of too exalted an order of being to be represented in private tombs. Such scenes are often stil found in tombs of later periods along with new scenes, for example, of the deceased worshiping the gods (Cat. 57b. Right wall: the deceased and his mother offering to various deities not represented. Left wall, upper register: the deceased before Osiris and four other funerary deities). The survival of the deceased was still in one way perceived as linked to the tomb and an existence similar to earthly life.

Tomb statues of deceased private persons were also made to help them secure eternal life. Like the corpse (Fig. 8) and all the representations so far discussed, they might become animated magically, for the Egyptians believed in the creative power of both words and images. For them, names and representations contained the essence of their subjects. Therefore, if a person's name were carved on a statue and the statue subjected to the proper rituals it could act on his or her behalf. A primary way in which a statue might function was as a medium through which the dead received offerings and other ministrations. Such offerings were, according to the inscriptions, made to the *Ka* of the deceased; and statues were associated with the *Ka*. Offerings were presented to statues (Cat. 20b) and sculptures are sometimes stated as having been made "to receive life."

In the Old Kingdom many tomb statues were placed in statue chambers, now called *serdabs,* connected to the other chambers of the tomb by slits in the wall through which the statue might see and through which incense might reach it. *Serdabs* were often located by false doors (Cat. 42), representations in stone of portals through which the deceased might come and go from the burial chamber behind and below, and before which offerings were made to him. In the Old Kingdom many tombs were furnished with a large number of statues of different types (Cat. 21-25), not all of which were placed in *serdabs* or in locations clearly marked as places for offering. Therefore, it is unlikely that their sole purpose was to receive offerings. Rather, just as the decoration of these tombs portrayed many aspects of the ideal earthly life of the deceased, so too did these statues.

Here as well as in art created for the temples, each representation makes a declaration about one aspect of existence which will render it alive and functioning for eternity. The art therefore has something of the nature of writing, for each statue or relief may be likened to a sentence or paragraph describing a single part of a complex subject which would require a chapter to describe in full detail. In fact, Egyptian art and writing are closely related as may clearly be seen by the manner in which reliefs and paintings often consist to a great extent of inscriptions.

The writing itself is an art form. Most hieroglyphs are representations of actual objects; and they were sometimes as elaborately carved or painted as were large–scale figures (Cat. 17 and 35). Their spacing was carefully worked out so as to form pleasing patterns. In general there was a tendency to arrange the hieroglyphs into square or rectangular groupings. The order in which the signs appeared in a word could be altered so as to give the word a more pleasing appearance.

The most striking analogy between art and writing is the arrangement of scenes in relief and painting into horizontal lines or registers. The figures within each register resemble words arranged in lines and sometimes a logical sequence of action can be "read" in these registers from top to bottom or bottom to top. Moreover, some of the figures represented are actually large–scale hieroglyphs.

The ancient Egyptian system of writing was partially phonetic and partially ideographic. Some signs were phonograms conveying sound values and others were ideograms which stood either for the thing of which they were a representation, or various abstract ideas. Ideograms often stood at the end of words after several phonograms. In this position they are called determinatives because, although sometimes it was originally the preceding phonograms that determined the specific sense conveyed by the ideogram, Egyptologists at first believed that their function was to indicate the specific word spelled by the phonograms.

These determinatives are important for an understanding of Egyptian art, for large–scale figures in relief and painting actually served as determinatives. The writing of names of men and women normally terminated in a figure of a man or woman. In Cat. 100, for example, the thirteenth sign from the right, a seated man, in the sixth line of the long inscription at the bottom of the stela, is the determinative for the name of the stela's owner. However, in the scene at the top of the stela where the owner's name appears just near the head of the large figure of the deceased, the determinative is omitted because the large figure itself functions as the determinative. Similarly, the seated figure of Wepemnofret (Cat. 17) also is surmounted by a writing of his name without a determinative. A similar function may be played by sculpture in the round. Thus the name of Kathesu on the side of his statue is written without a determinative (Cat. 21). Sometimes the forms of large sculptures resembled those of hieroglyphs. For example, the type of squatting deity represented by the tenth sign from the right in the first line of the long inscription on Cat. 100 is used for depictions of numerous deities in both relief and statuary. A sunk relief of the goddess Maat in this pose is held by the king in Cat. 107; and statues of the goddess in the same attitude are known.

The orientation of writing had an effect upon the composition of the decoration on monuments such as stelae. Inasmuch as the texts are generally to be read from right to left and the figures take their orientation from that of the inscriptions whose signs face the front of the line, the principal personnages represented would generally face right (Cat. 17, 29, 30, 31, 42, 100, and 109). Moreover, if they were the only figures represented they would be placed in the left part of the decorated field because the Egyptians had an aversion to compositions in which figures faced outward from the edge of a decorated surface.

Another relationship between art and writing may be seen in certain uses of sunk relief. This characteristically Egyptian sculptural technique, in which the background was not cut away, was probably developed and used for several reasons. It was faster and cheaper to execute than raised relief and so it may have been used when time and resources were a primary concern. It may have come to be employed on exterior surfaces because it was less liable to damage than raised relief and also because the shadows cast in its hollows would cause the representations to stand out strongly and not wash out visually in the bright Egyptian sun. Sunk relief was, however, first used for inscriptions and later may sometimes have been used because it had become associated with writing. In some tombs where human figures in both sunk and raised relief function as determinatives for their names, the figures in raised relief are larger in relation to the hieroglyphs they accompany than are the figures in sunk relief; or, unlike the figures in sunk relief, they are separated from their inscriptions by a line. In other words, the figures appear to be executed in sunk relief if they are perceived as hieroglyphs.

Other examples of the relationship of art to writing deserve mention because of the importance of this subject to an understanding of Egyptian art. The figures of the three gods at the top of the back pillar in Cat. 103b represent the Theban triad of Amun-Re, his wife Mut, and their son Khonsu-pakhered. Though they are separated by a line from the following inscriptions, each deity is the first hieroglyph in one of the columns of text. For example, without the figure of Amun the first column to the left would read "... Re, lord of heaven ...." As is pointed out in the entries for Cat. 54 and 104, both reliefs and sculpture in the round could simultaneously function as representations of one thing and writings of another; and in Fig. 9 the falcon which at first appears to be a representation of the god Horus as in Fig. 3 is actually a three–dimensional hieroglyph in the king's Horus name usually written in relief (Fig. 2).

This relationship between two– and three–dimensional art is especially common after the Middle Kingdom. The Ptolemaic statue of Nes–thoth (Cat. 108) could have been shown holding a three–dimensional figure of the baboon–shaped deity before him, but there would have been no difference in meaning between a statue and the sunk relief figure carved on his robe. If art were to make a statement, what mattered was that the statement be made. It could be rendered by means of large figures, or stated in the inscriptions. Sometimes, as in the case of Cat. 35 where the cobra hieroglyph for the names of a goddess offers signs of power toward the king's Horus name, the writing itself could depict the action stated.

Fig. 9. Statue of King Pepy II with his Horus name. Dynasty VI. Brooklyn, The Brooklyn Museum.

The declarations made by the art are more concerned with the typical than the specific, with the eternally valid rather than with historical events which happen only once. For example, the scenes on the temple walls showing the king offering to the gods, with few exceptions, seldom depict historical reality. Rather they represent one part of the king's reciprocal relationship with the gods, his theoretical daily performance of their cult rituals. Even scenes such as those of the king defeating Egypt's enemies do not, as we have noted, necessarily depict actual events; and when they do represent specific royal achievement it is as often commemorated by a heraldic and conventional pose of triumph embodying the essential religious significance of the feat as by a detailed narration of the events involved.

Historical reality is also generally missing from the decoration of private tombs, where what is represented is primarily the ideal state of existence of the deceased. In such scenes, eternally valid, the specific and the momentary had little place, although occasionally historical achievements of the deceased might sometimes enter the iconography.

Much the same may be said about statuary. This is one reason why few Egyptian sculptures are true portraits by the modern definition of that term: a representation showing the actual features of the subject as well as conveying his or her character or personality. Portraiture was not necessary to the purposes for which Egyptian statues were made, and some of those purposes mitigated against the creation of true portraiture.

In the first place, inasmuch as all that was needed to identify a sculpture with its owner was the presence of that person's name, there was no reason why a statue had to resemble its owner to function for him. In fact, the survival of one's name alone might ensure immortality; and sculptures were created so that the name of the owner might live, as the inscription on the statue of Pedimahes indicates (Cat. 94). Therefore, one person might appropriate a statue made for another by the simple expedient of substituting his or her name for that of the original owner. Similarly, one might do harm to an individual by erasing his name from a relief or statue or by damaging the image magically associated with him.

Secondly, the permanent had to take precedence over the transitory. If a sculpture represented only one of the various manifestations of the multifaceted form and essence of its subject, it was the true and permanent form and essence which must show through. Impermanent physical actuality must take second place. In this sense, even though the terms ideal and idealized are used elsewhere in this book, the Egyptian artist creating a sculpture showing its subject as having a perfectly healthy, young, and muscular body, was not creating an ideal form. Such physiques were not conceptions of absolute perfection existing only in the mind. Nor were they forms conforming to a conception of absolute perfection. Instead they were eternally valid images of the essence of their owners. If physical infirmities or defects and the decrepitude of old age seldom were depicted, that is because they were transitory features of life and not part of one's essence. So too, fleeting characteristics of the subject, such as emotion, were not generally represented. And yet, within this framework there was room for some degree of verisimilitude in the art. Although a person's sculptures were not meant to render his exact appearance or personality, since there was no need for them to do so for the sculptures to accomplish their primary tasks, there was also no reason why they should *not* resemble their owners in some ways.

To be sure, the sculptures made for a king early in his reign might have facial features resembling those of his predecessor until a new official image was developed; and various facial types might exist for the same king. However, the sculptures made for a king often have enough in common for us to assume that they partially reflected his actual appearance. This is most clearly visible in the art created for King Akhenaten, because most of his sculptures have certain individual features of both face and body in common (Cat. 62-66). Nevertheless, even here, during a time when art reproduced nature more closely than in other periods, the variations between the representations of the king prevent us from determining precisely what he looked like and clearly demonstrate how little Egyptian art had to resemble physical actuality.

Individualistic faces and faces with one or two individual features (Cat. 20 and 54) sometimes occur in private statuary; and, as in royal sculptures, it is likely that some such works bear a resemblance to the actual appearance of their owners. However, in the overwhelming number of instances where more than one sculpture of a person has survived (Cat. 54) the faces of the various works bear little specific resemblance to each other but rather reflect the facial features current in the art of the time. In general, as a comparison between a royal (Cat. 40) and a private work (Cat. 41) of the Middle Kingdom indicates, the features were dependent upon those in the royal sculptures. The gods were regularly given physiognomies based on those of the king. For example, in the triads made for King Mycerinus the facial features vary from sculpture to sculpture, but within each triad the two deities have faces resembling that of the accompanying figure of the king (Fig. 10).

It may be argued that the concept of Maat mitigated against the creation of true portraiture in that the artists would emphasize what was typical and representative in the physiognomy of Egyptians, who were within the world order as opposed to foreigners outside that order. The "foreignness" of the latter was frequently rendered in an exaggerated fashion to emphasize their difference from the Egyptians (Cat. 76).

At any rate, it is significant that portraiture only really developed in the latter periods of Egyptian history, after individuals had attained more direct and personal relationship with the gods, when political developments produced an obvious contrast between the ideal state of things and actuality, and when, among the educated, there arose a greater degree of skepticism than ever before about survival after death. The inscriptions on statues of this period became more personal and directly aimed at the observer; and they appear to indicate a feeling that the immortality one could be sure of consisted in the continuance of one's good name on earth and remembrance by posterity. These conceptions, more individualistic than former beliefs, would have been more fertile ground from which portraiture might grow.

If individuality and sometimes true portraiture are occasionally found in Egyptian art, it should be noted that it is generally limited to figures' faces, and not to the representation of the entire body. This in no small

Fig. 10. Triad of King Mycerinus, the goddess Hathor, and a goddess of one of the administrative districts of Egypt. From the King's funerary temple at Giza. Dynasty IV. Boston, Museum of Fine Arts.

part derives from the Egyptian artists' methods of constructing human figures.

The Egyptians solved the problem of how to scale the component parts of the human figure by establishing a canon of proportions based on their system of measurement. The body might be divided into a certain number of units—eighteen prior to the Later Period—with each part being a definite number (or fractions thereof) of those units. Such a procedure could have resulted in unnatural figures. However, inasmuch as the Egyptian measurements were based on parts of the human body to begin with and the parts of the human body normally display certain proportional relationships with each other, their system resulted in the standardization of natural proportions and in the elimination of natural variations. The way the artists executed their works according to this system was simple. They covered the surface to be carved or painted with a grid of squares and drew their preliminary sketches so that each part of the figure extended along the predetermined proper number of squares.

The canon was not always used. Considerable deviations from its norm do occur, especially in representations of lesser personnages such as servants and prisoners. Nevertheless, it was used often enough to insure, even in works of lesser quality, conformation to certain standards. The proportioning of figures according to a canon may well have arisen from the desire to create figures which were universally valid and hence efficacious for their magical task; but it also probably reflects the influence of their religious beliefs on the Egyptians' aesthetic sensibilities. The concept of a universe functioning by the harmonious interaction and relationship of its separate parts may well have given rise to the perception of the harmonious as beautiful. Such a harmony based on measurements often extended beyond the construction of single figures into the composition of entire scenes.

In order that the reader may see that such proportions exist in art, it is appropriate here to point out a few interesting details about some pieces illustrated in this book. In Cat. 29 the greatest expansion of the lateral space covered by the female figure, from the rear edge of her wig to the tip of her toe, is almost exactly equal to the greatest width of the pile of offerings to the right. In Cat. 42 the greatest width of the pile of offerings, excluding the lotus plant floating before the man's face, is almost precisely one–third the width of the field enclosed by the texts and one–half the height of the field with the seated figure's waist coming halfway between the bottom and top. The distance from the left edge of the field to the front edge of the larger figure's foot is virtually the same as that from the right edge of the field to the rear of his chair. In Cat. 109 the greatest width covered by the figure to the right—that from the rear of his shoulder to the tip of the censer he holds—is almost exactly one–half the greatest width—from the rear of the woman's shoulder to the front edge of the man's toes—of the group of two figures to the right. It is also approximately one–third the width of the field flanked by the scepters. Similarly, in Fig. 6, the figures of Horus and Thoth each extend across one–third of the decorated field. Measurements such as these cannot be totally fortuitous; but it must be emphasized that the compositions are not slavishly mechanical or rigidly symmetrical. Symmetrical compositions did, of course, exist, but they were not the rule. Compositions around the central axis are common (Cat. 100), and because the Egyptians preferred self–contained compositions they liked to terminate decorated surfaces with figures facing inward toward the center as well as framing them with bands and inscriptions. But on either side of the central axis the decoration is seldom identical. The same is true of statuary where, for example, one shoulder may be higher than another and the features on either side of the face somewhat different.

Sometimes the compositions are symbolic as, for example, in Cat. 101. Here the deceased is associated with the solar cycle in two ways. First, he is represented in the same boat as the solar deities. Secondly, a triangle formed by connecting the centers of the three large solar disks would, if flipped over to form a rhombus, have its fourth apex in the head of the deceased, thus clearly linking him to this cycle of birth and rebirth. This part of the composition is, therefore, both geometric and symbolic. Another means of graphic symbolism is also displayed in Cat. 101 in the way the long hieroglyph for sky over the register with the boat is tilted so that it is higher by the rising sun and lower by the setting sun. Stelae as a whole, in fact, are sometimes symbolic representations of the world, as may be seen in their decoration with a sign for heaven supported by scepters and solar disk from which hang *uraei* wearing the crowns of Upper and Lower Egypt (Cat. 101 and 109).

The drawing of human figures according to a canon of proportions and the building up of scenes from their component elements are, in a manner akin to the construction of words and sentences from individual hieroglyphs, dependent upon the fact that the Egyptian artists rendered what they were depicting part for part as it really was. Accidental features are ignored and each part is rendered as if seen frontally. Although the entire figure is not complete, each part is represented as completely as possible with the most characteristic view of the part rendered.

The Egyptian artist did not, therefore, normally draw things in perspective, that is as seen from a single viewpoint and visually foreshortened. Faced with the task, for example, of representing a building, the artist would generally, but not always (Fig. 4), render it from a combination of frontal and aerial views. To convey their appearance, doors would be drawn as seen frontally and walls as if seen from above to give the plan and allow persons and objects to be shown within them (Fig. 8, 11, and Cat. 67). Landscape elements such as ponds and rivers were often rendered in aerial view (Fig. 4 and Cat. 52). Most compositions therefore give an impression of flatness, although the overlapping of figures (Fig. 11) and sometimes the staggering of overlapping rows of figures, with each figure rising partially above the one before it (Fig. 4), can give a sense of depth.

In two–dimensional art this method of drawing also resulted in a series of conventions for the rendering of the human figure. These, like the canon of proportions, helped standardize such representations to a considerable degree. The face is seen in profile but the eye is frontal. Shoulders are generally seen frontally as are hands; but arms, legs, and feet are normally rendered as if seen in profile. The torso is not quite in profile for, although only one breast is shown, the navel is visible. Because they preferred to show the inner profile of the foot with the arch visible, most figures have

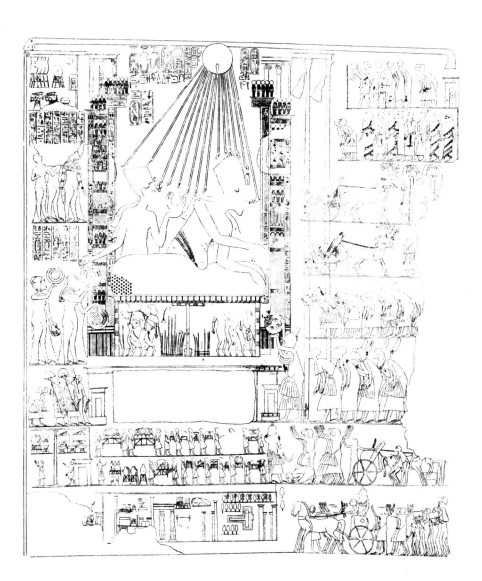

Fig. 11. King Akhenaten and Queen Nefertiti rewarding an official with necklaces of gold. Drawing of a relief in a private tomb at Tell el Amarna. Dynasty XVIII.

two similar feet, not a right and a left foot. Figures also often have two of the same hand.

Such a manner of seeing and drawing is a delimiting mode of expression. Just as each part of a figure is seen separately and discreetly, so also are whole figures generally clear and self–contained forms. This is true of statuary as well as relief and painting, for the former was conceived in the same manner with each of the four sides seen separately.

It must not be inferred from this that Egyptian art is not naturalistic, for almost all works are based on natural forms. In fact, the use of natural forms for architecture, furniture, and decorative objects is a major charac-teristic of art made in the Nile Valley. Chairs might have animal–shaped (Fig. 2 and Cat. 17) and even plant–shaped (Cat. 96a) legs, while plant shapes might be given to various types of vessels (Cat. 52) and other imple-ments (Cat. 75 and 82), including mirrors (Cat. 31). Human forms were also popular, as may be seen in objects such as mirrors with handles in the form of girls (Cat. 72) clappers in the form of hands (Cat. 51), and censers ending in hands (Cat. 109). That these forms sometimes (Cat. 51 and 109) were appropriate to the actual function of the object (Cat. 51 and 109) is also characteristic of the art.

Naturalism was tempered by the Egyptians' aesthetic sense which displays a preference for rectangular and cubic forms. The proportional relationships, discussed above, between elements in scenes were really those between the rectangles one might inscribe around the greatest height and width of figures and objects; and balanced against these are the rectangular areas of inscription. In the sculpture in the round, most statues retain to a considerable extent a block–like appearance. This is enhanced by the presence of elements such as back pillars and back slabs. However, it must be remembered that, when made of wood, the statues could be considerably less cubic. Moreover, the areas left between the limbs in stone statuary were sometimes painted black or white, probably to characterize them as negative space.

If Egyptian art displayed a general preference for rectangular forms and compositions based on horizontals and verticals, it might also use curved lines; in the New Kingdom, delight was taken in composition based in no small part on curvilinear forms (Fig. 1, 4, 11, and Cat. 58). If the art tended to prefer static forms, motion might also be rendered. Sometimes this was achieved by the simple expedient of showing an object frozen in a pose of motion (Fig. 4 and 12), but it could also be rendered by repetition, as in the dots streaming from the sun in Cat. 101. If simple, distinct forms were generally preferred, figures might on other occasions overlap to a considerable extent.

Fig. 12. King Djoser performing a ritual of rejuvenation. Relief from his funerary complex at Saqqara. Dynasty III.

It must always be borne in mind that while certain elements of Egyptian art remained fairly constant throughout its long history, there was a great deal of change. Moreover, considerable variations existed even during a single period. As we have seen, changes in subject matter tended to come slowly and the old could coexist with the new. But each age's concept of the divine order was slightly different from that of other periods, and each age had its own ideal of beauty as is reflected in the variations in facial features, costumes, coiffures, decorative motifs, use of landscape elements and color schemes.

It must not be thought that Egyptian art, simply because much of it was made for the tomb, was not meant to be seen or appreciated. Only parts of the tombs, such as the burial chamber, were inaccessible; and visitors were encouraged to enter to say prayers and make offerings. Some of the tomb's reliefs were therefore visible; and even in the Old Kingdom, as noted before, not all statues were sealed in *serdabs*. In later periods a great deal of the sculpture stood visible in temples along with parts of the temple's decoration.

From the New Kingdom we have visitors' inscriptions on famous old monuments; and when Hatshepsut built her temple at Deir el Bahri over the tomb of Queen Neferu (Cat. 32-33b), a new entrance to the later monument was provided. These graffiti indicate that the purpose of such visits combined antiquarian interest and piety, for the monuments most visited had become shrines. However, an aesthetic interest seems to be indicated as well.

Finally, it must be emphasized that while most of the art objects preserved for us are from tombs and temples, the Egyptians in life also loved to surround themselves with beauty in the form of jewelry and minor art objects, and also adorned their homes with wall paintings. These too changed in style from period to period and helped give Egyptian art a great variety within its basic unity.

Sources of Illustrations

Fig. 1 from Calverly, A. M., *The Temple of King Sethos I at Abydos,* Vol. II (London, 1935), pl. 30, courtesy The Egypt Exploration Society; *Fig. 2* from *Encyclopédie photographique de l'art,* Vol. I (Paris, 1935), p. 4, courtesy Editions "Tel"; *Figs. 3 and 12* from Lange, K., and Hirmer, M., *Egypt: Architecture, Sculpture, Painting in Three Thousand Years,* 4th ed. (London and New York, 1968), pls. IV and 15, courtesy Hirmer Verlag; *Fig. 4* from Wreszinski, W., *Atlas zur altaegyptischen Kulturgeschichte,* Vol. II (Leipzig, 1935), pl. 84, courtesy J. C. Hinrichs; *Fig. 5* reproduced by the kindness of the Ashmolean Museum, Oxford; *Fig. 7* from Lepsius, C. R., *Denkmaeler aus Aegypten und Aethiopien nach den Zeichnungen der von Seiner Majestaet dem Koenige von Preussen Friedrich Wilhelm IV nach diesen Laendern gesendeten und in den Jahren 1842-1845 ausgefuehrten wissenschaftlichen Expedition* . . . Part 3, *Denkmaeler des Neuen Reiches* (Berlin, 1848-1859), pl. 235; *Fig. 8* from Le Page Renouf, P., *The Egyptian Book of the Dead,* Vol. I (London, 1893), pl. II; *Fig. 10* reproduced by the kindness of the Museum of Fine Arts, Boston; *Fig. 11* from Davies, N. de G., *The Rock Tombs of El Amarna.* Part 2, *The Tombs of Panehesy and Meryre II.* Egypt Exploration Society, Archaeological Survey of Egypt. Memoir, 14 (London, 1905), pl. xxxiii, courtesy The Egypt Exploration Society.

I. The Predynastic and Early Dynastic Periods

Egypt's prehistoric era ended with the appearance of writing and the rise to power in Upper and Lower Egypt of the kings of Dynasty I, sometime between 3100 and 2950 B.C. From that time the country was ruled, except in periods of internal weakness, by successive dynasties of kings. All prehistoric Egyptian cultures are therefore predynastic, the name Predynastic Period being specifically reserved for the approximately thousand years prior to dynastic times because this period provides evidence for cultures at once distinct from those preceding them and giving rise to later, historical Egyptian civilization.

Gaps still exist in our knowledge of the Predynastic Period, especially in Lower Egypt, because of the absence of written records, limitations in the quantity and variety of archaeological material, and difficulties involved in interpreting the available evidence.

However, excavations in Upper Egypt have yielded material from which it has been possible to reconstruct a sequence of three closely related and partially overlapping cultural phases, terminating in Dynasty I. Each phase has been named after the site producing the first or most important evidence for it. The names used here are Badarian, Amratian, and Gerzean. To stress their continuity, Amratian and Gerzean are also called Naqada I and II, respectively—Naqada II being divided into early and late subphases. In recent years it has been argued that Badarian is wholly contemporary with Amratian, and that the resulting cultural sequence should be divided into three phases: Naqada I-III, each with several subphases. At present, the beginning of the Predynastic Period is generally placed before 4000 B.C.

The three phases of Upper Egyptian Predynastic culture were basically alike: the people of Badarian, Amratian, and Gerzean times led a settled existence based on agriculture and the domestication of animals. They buried their dead in similar manners, sometimes with typologically and stylistically similar objects—including pottery, jewelry, slate palettes, and figures of animals and humans. For example, black-topped pottery, found in Badarian graves, was still made in Gerzean times (Cat. 2). It constitutes one of the clear links between the early cultures of Egypt and Nubia to the south. Amratian slate palettes in the form of animals differ very little from later Gerzean ones (Cat. 7); and Gerzean pins of the type represented by Cat. 8 were known in Amratian times. Variations on the type of female figure with raised arms (Cat. 1), an Egyptian version of a figure type encountered throughout much of the ancient world, are also found in both periods. Stone vessels were made throughout the Predynastic Period, and in Gerzean times became more common and sometimes more elaborate (Cat. 9), but most luxury vessels were of pottery (Cat. 2, 3, 4, 5 and 6). It is these latter decorated pots which represent the beginning of Egyptian painting, just as the small Predynastic figures of animals and humans constitute the beginning of Egyptian sculpture in the round.

If the three cultural phases of the Predynastic Period retained certain basic features until the end of that era, they were not static.

The appearance in Amratian cemeteries of a few large, rectangular graves among the smaller oval ones heralds the early stages of a social and economic stratification which was carried much further in the succeeding period. The Gerzean culture, unlike the Badarian and Amratian, spread into Lower Egypt. This physical expansion was accompanied by population growth, greater exploitation of the natural resources, and a developed unity and organization of society. It was also accompanied by the clear signs of increased contact with the more advanced civilizations of the Near East.

The most important factor in this socio-economic change, however, appears to have been the rise of that most central and enduring of Egyptian institutions, kingship. The organization of Upper Egypt under a single strong ruler or—perhaps until later in the Gerzean Period, several rulers—would have made the other changes possible.

From the middle of the Gerzean Period on, we have what may be called royal art. Later in the Gerzean Period the artistic manifestations of kingship become numerous. It should be pointed out that while not all Gerzean art directly reflects the cultural changes of the times, the effects of these changes were nevertheless far-reaching. For example, there is a shift in luxury pottery from vessels with open forms, such as bowls with flaring rims, their interiors decorated with light-on-dark designs (Cat. 4), to vessels of more closed form, such as bellied or shouldered jars, ornamented on their exteriors with dark-on-light decoration (Cat. 5 and 6). This represents a change of artistic taste at least partially dependent upon economic factors. The change in color was due to a change in the clay used; and it has been argued that these pots were made only in a few localities where this clay was worked. Furthermore, the large number of these painted pots and the standardization of their form and decoration—Cat. 5 and 6 are by no means unique—indicates they were the product of "mass production." This would have influenced the taste of the time and helped spread it over a wide area.

The first clear manifestation of royal art is also the first known wall painting in Egypt. It occurs in a tomb of a Predynastic king at Hierakonpolis. The painting displays the same loose type of composition as in contemporary Gerzean pottery (Cat. 6), so different from the more compact and geometrically organized designs imposed on Amratian pots by the need to decorate a circular interior surface. But unlike the decoration of the pottery, features of this painting, such as the placing of some figures on base lines and the motif of a larger figure smiting smaller figures, anticipate developments in the numerous royal objects made at the end of the period.

These later creations include new types of objects, such as large sculptures for temples (Cat. 11). More common are objects of older, Predynastic type, such as slate palettes. These are now made for dedication in temples rather than for burials and are covered with figures in relief, the first flowering of this sculptural form in Egypt. Some are decorated solely with animals whose symbolism escapes us. Others commemorate battles connected with the unification of the country or portray religious ceremonies associated with those events. Sometimes the action represented is performed by symbols of the king, his allies, or the gods—a mode of representation common in Egyptian art. In this early period the symbols are usually animals. The king, however, is also shown in human form, wearing recognizable royal regalia, in poses commonly found in later royal reliefs. Furthermore, figures are drawn in the soon to be traditional Egyptian combination of frontal and profile views, on different scales indicative of status, and resting on base lines. In a few cases an object's decoration is arranged in horizontal registers, and some figures are accompanied by identifying labels.

This art stands firmly in the traditions of the art of Dynasty I so that the distinction between the late Predynastic and Early Dynastic Periods is a somewhat misleading convention. The unification of the country and its consolidation certainly took more than one reign to accomplish, as the art clearly indicates. For this reason, the transitional phase between the two periods is often termed Dynasty O.

Despite the fact that its beginning cannot be clearly distinguished from the preceding period and that its end is characterized by the production of art anticipating that of the Old Kingdom (Dynasties III-VIII), the Early Dynastic Period (Dynasties I-II: 3100/2950 B.C.–2635 B.C.) is still a distinct chronological and artistic epoch. It was a dynamic age of artistic experimentation which at the same time betrayed distinct signs of the conservatism common to Egyptian culture.

The large tombs of royalty and aristocrats which appear at the beginning of Dynasty I are the first monumental architecture known in Egypt. Built of mud brick, with facades adorned with niches and buttresses in imitation of the design of the large wood and reed residences of the king and his court, the tombs, like the houses, were based upon architectural forms first developed by Egypt's neighbors in the Near East.

With the appearance of this monumental architecture came the appearance of monumental sculpture, some of which was made for the tombs. The stela of King Djet of early Dynasty I (Fig. 2), for example, comes from a tomb he built at Abydos. The connection between tomb and stela is emphasized by the fact that the hieroglyph for the king's name: the snake (below the falcon proclaiming him as an incarnation of the god Horus), is placed above a representation of the type of facade common to both royal palaces and tombs. The bold and somewhat stiff forms of this relief, displaying a minimum of modeling, relate it to the reliefs on the slate palettes discussed above. The simplicity of its design, however, is a new departure from the generally more complicated composition of slate palettes, while its unmechanical, carefully balanced asymmetrical composition links it to the best works of Egyptian art of all periods.

Stelae of the same type were made for later kings of Dynasties I and II, but they show a decline in quality both in their cruder carving and less spacious compositions. From the reign of King Khasekhemuwy, the last ruler of Dynasty II, is preserved a granite door jamb whose reliefs, although badly damaged, show that by the end of the Early Dynastic Period artists were capable of carving raised reliefs in hard stones such as granite. The style and iconography clearly link them to the art of the Old Kingdom.

The same is true in the realm of sculpture in the round, as evidenced by the statue of King Khasekhem (Fig. 5), either Khasekhemuwy's predecessor or Khasekhemuwy himself. His pose, and the emphasis of the cubic shape link this work to the art of Dynasty III, some of which barely shows a more developed skill in the carving of stone. The contorted prisoners incised on the base still link the piece to the less formally ordered work of earlier times. Unfortunately, we cannot trace the development of stone sculpture in the round in the Early Dynastic Period for too few works have been preserved. But it should be pointed out that, no matter what the cumulative achievement by the end of the period, even more dramatic sculptures were being made in other materials. In a chapel connected to a tomb of the reign of Ka'a, last king of Dynasty I, were found the feet and bases of two wooden male statues. These statues were two-thirds lifesize and represented the person portrayed as striding with left leg advanced, the pose most often assumed by standing sculptures of men (Cat. 12) in later periods of Egyptian art. They would also appear to be our first example of the use of sculptures of the deceased in tomb chapels, a practice which later became common.

There were also dramatic developments in the contemporary reliefs of private, although distinctly upper class personages. From Dynasties I and II are preserved a number of tomb stelae which show the deceased seated at a table with offerings. Unlike later fine stelae of the Old Kingdom, their hieroglyphs are not neatly aligned on true horizontal and vertical axes, and both figures and representations are crowded together. The figures themselves are often oddly proportioned with large heads and thin, stunted legs. If the artists had not yet perfected their technical skills and arrived at a general canon of proportions for the human figure, these stelae show, just as do the wooden feet mentioned above, that elements of artistic iconography were already being codified. In subject matter these stelae are the direct ancestors of many funerary stelae of later periods (Cat. 17).

Cat. 1. Female figure with birdlike head. Although both human and animal figures were treated with varying degrees of realism and abstraction during all periods of Egyptian art, some Predynastic art is more abstract than most art of later times. In this figure the simplified forms of the body stress its gender while the elongation and curve of the arms and hands—stylistic devices sometimes later used in a more naturalistic manner for similar purposes—accentuate the gesture made and add to the elegance of the whole.

The purpose of this and other related female figures is uncertain, but as they generally come from burials it is assumed that they were intended to benefit magically the persons with whom they were interred. Such sculptures have been interpreted as representations of the spirits of the deceased, as eternal concubines for the dead, as fertility charms, as images of deities, as ritual dancers, and as mourners. Given the difficulty of determining their meaning or meanings in the absence of any inscriptional evidence, the question of their function is likely to remain open.

This figure has been attributed to both the Amratian and Gerzean Periods, more often to the former than to the latter. Pottery. Height 33.8 cm.

1

Pottery, both painted and unpainted, was the most common art form during the Predynastic Period with some vessels ranking among the era's finest creations. In later times, when stone was the preferred material for luxury vessels (Cat. 13), far less fine pottery was made; and, with the exception of New Kingdom work (Cat. 58), it was only during the Predynastic Period that the painting of pottery was an important medium for artistic expression.

Vessels with blackened tops and interior surfaces (Cat. 2) were made throughout the Predynastic Period in Egypt; in Nubia their manufacture continued for a far longer period of time. Vessels with red polished surfaces were also made during both the Amratian and Gerzean Periods and sometimes they were embellished with incised decoration (Cat. 3)—a phenomenon not limited to this class of pottery.

Among the painted vessels geometric and figurative motifs were utilized during both the Amratian (Cat. 4) and Gerzean Periods (Cat. 5 and 6). The motifs were not, however, identical during the two periods, and the figurative motifs are more often found on Gerzean pottery than on Amratian pottery.

Although the typological and stylistic divisions between Amratian and Gerzean pottery are not absolute, white cross-lined painting on a red ground (Cat. 4) is primarily characteristic of the Amratian Period whereas the reverse value scheme—red decoration on a buff ground—is typical of the Gerzean Period (Cat. 5 and 6).

2

Cat. 2. Red jar with black interior and top. The two-value scheme of decoration was achieved through an unequal oxidation of the surface. Gerzean Period. Pottery. Height 24.5 cm.

Cat. 3. Polished red jar. The incised rendering of a bull is related to other prehistoric Egyptian drawings but it is also linked to much of later Egyptian art by its emphasis upon outline and the essential features of its subject. Gerzean Period. Pottery. Height 25.2 cm.

3

Cat. 4. Red bowl. The interior surface is adorned with a geometric pattern of white lines. The design is admirably suited to the bowl's circular shape. Amratian Period. Pottery. Height 7.9 cm.

Cat. 5. Buff jar with roll handles. The vessel is decorated with red vertical bands filled with zigzag lines resembling a later stylistic convention for water. Gerzean Period. Pottery. Height 12.0 cm.

Cat. 6. Buff jar. The stylized red representations of boat, flamingos, and other motifs are not quite united in a true landscape. The boat with its emblem may depict a type used for the transportation of goods, of a deceased person, or of a statue of a deity. Gerzean Period. Pottery. Height 23.0 cm.

4

5

6

On the basis of style, typology, or archaeological context, these five objects are attributable to the late Predynastic Period. They reflect several aspects of the art and religion of Egypt at the dawn of its history, not the least interesting of which is the transition from the old to the new.

Three of the pieces are more closely linked to the art which preceded them than to that which followed. Slate palettes were made during most of the Predynastic Period, and the fish-shaped palette (Cat. 7) is of a type popular throughout the Gerzean Period. The ivory pin (Cat. 8) is also primarily related to objects made prior to Dynasty I and represents a general type of adornment of the Amratian Period. The stone frog-shaped vessel (Cat. 9), on the other hand, represents a specific class of object which, although animal-shaped vessels were known earlier, had a far more limited chronological range. All three pieces display the almost constant Egyptian tendency to give objects biomorphic forms or to decorate them with motifs drawn from nature.

The slate dog or jackal (Cat. 10) and the lion's head (Cat. 11) more clearly point to the future. Both stand near the beginning of the line of larger stone animal sculptures made throughout Egyptian history.

Cat. 10, though not a palette, may nevertheless be related to such objects which it resembles both in its thinness and material. A two-sided figure rather than a complete sculpture in the round, its proportions are longer and squatter than those of later representations of this animal.

Cat. 11 is dated to the very end of the Predynastic Period on

Cat. 7. Palette in the form of a fish. Palettes like this were sometimes used for grinding eyepaint. This piece, once enlivened with inlays, has a hole for suspension. Slate. Length 18.1 cm.

Cat. 8. Pin with head in the form of a bird. The eyes may once have been inlaid; there are traces of black paste in the incised chevrons and crosshatching. From the same burial as Cat. 9. Ivory. Height 16.0 cm.

Cat. 9. Frog-shaped vessel. The eyes are inlaid with white stone beads and the body markings are indicated by chips of lapis lazuli. From the same burial as Cat. 8. Limestone. Length 9.2 cm.

7

9

8

the basis of stylistic similarities to other works either probably or certainly of the period. Apart from its large size, its most striking feature is the highly simplified modeling. It is not until the late Predynastic Period that we have ample evidence for large scale reliefs and stone sculptures in the round. The reliefs, unlike the sculptures in the round, exhibit numerous details generally rendered by means of incised lines and, to a far lesser extent, modeling. The simplified but sophisticated treatment of Cat. 11 may derive from the hardness of its stone; however, as softer stones could also be worked in a simplified manner, it may also be partly a matter of taste. Certainly the use of soft materials did not always call forth detailed naturalistic renderings (Cat. 1).

Cat. 7-10 come from burials, and it is probable that they were meant to function magically for the deceased. The pin, a treasured possession during life, would serve for adornment in the hereafter; and the palette—too small for practical use—for the grinding of eyepaint. But it is possible that the palette and frog-shaped vessel were also made for a magical purpose not directly related to their normal uses. We have good reason to believe that in later periods "practical" objects such as spoons (Cat. 75 and 82) and bowls (Cat. 52) were carved in the form of, or decorated with, motifs possessing magical powers of benefit to their owners. We also know that both frogs and fish were associated with various deities and were potent symbols of the creative forces of life and rebirth. It therefore seems probable that the deceased persons buried with Cat. 8 and 9 believed these objects would command for them powers necessary for life after death.

It is tempting to see in Cat. 10, an object with no apparent practical function, an early representation of one of the deities associated with the dead who became manifest in the form of a jackal or dog. If so, its owner, by being buried with a figure of the god, hoped to command magically that deity's power on his own behalf.

As for the lion's head (Cat. 11), although its exact provenance is not known, it must have come from a temple. The lion, a symbol of great power, was traditionally associated with numerous gods; it is possible that the figure of a recumbent lion from which this head came was an early cult image. However, as lion figures are commonly used to guard sacred precincts, it is more likely that our lion, rather than representing the deity worshiped in a temple, was made to ward off evil from the earthly home of such a god or goddess.

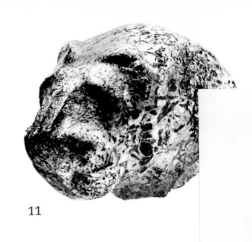

11

Cat. 10. Figure of a jackal or dog. The eyes of this animal—perhaps a representation of a funerary deity —were formerly inlaid. Slate. Length 40.0 cm.

Cat. 11. Head from a large sculpture of a lion which served as a guardian figure for a temple. Black and white granite. Height 24.8 cm.

10

II. The Old Kingdom And The First Intermediate Period

The royal and aristocratic art evolved in the Late Predynastic and Early Dynastic Periods came to fruition early in the Old Kingdom: Dynasties III-VIII, 2635 to 2135 B.C.

The capital of the now united country was founded at Memphis, just to the south of modern Cairo at the juncture of the broad Egyptian Delta and the narrow Nile Valley of Middle and Upper Egypt. That city became the center of Egypt's political and economic power. It also rapidly became the artistic fountainhead of the country—as was understandable in a land where so much of the wealth and power was concentrated in the hands of the king and of a small circle of courtiers and officials. We have little information about the art and architecture of most areas of Egypt outside the Memphite region in Dynasties III and IV, but it would seem certain that by Dynasty III the most important monuments were those erected in the cemeteries of the capital.

It was in the Old Kingdom that the Egyptian kings enjoyed their greatest power and the country its most centralized control. The apogee of royal power appears to have been reached in early Dynasty IV (2570–2450 B.C.) and was fairly well maintained until after early Dynasty V (2450–2290 B.C.). Thereafter, the size and, to some extent, the quality of the royal monuments diminished. At the same time the higher administrative offices became available to others besides the king's relatives who, since at least the beginning of Dynasty IV, had traditionally held these posts. In addition, the great building projects of Dynasty IV had produced a considerable number of craftsmen who could satisfy the needs of a new class. From this point on a larger number of people, though still a small part of the total population, were able to have tombs built which were decorated with relief and sculpture. Not all these of course were of the finest quality; some in fact were quite small monuments, often crudely carved. However, they were created for enduring religious purposes, and they were situated in the vicinity of royal monuments which might serve as direct or indirect inspiration. Thus, a more or less traditional style and some degree of technical skill were maintained, at least in the area of the capital, until the end of Dynasty VI (2290–2155 B.C.).

In the provinces, certainly in the South as evidence proves, the situation was somewhat different. With the expansion of the government a certain degree of decentralization became inevitable. While major provincial tombs were rare in Dynasty IV, they increased in number in Dynasty V, and became common in Dynasty VI. The district administrators, whose tombs these were, kept close ties with the central court, and many of the craftsmen they employed must have been from Memphis, just as sculptures were imported from that city. Many of these provincial monuments came increasingly to be produced by local talent, reflecting their cultural ambience. Unusual subject matter appeared from time to time in the decoration of these tombs, while both reliefs and statuary revealed certain crudities of contour and modeling. These factors of subject and style were not always artistically unfortunate. They added lively touches sometimes lacking in more purely traditional and polished works, and they also, as we shall see, were important preludes to the art of the First Intermediate Period and, later still, the Middle Kingdom.

With Dynasty III, Egypt may in a sense be said to have entered its long artistic and architectural age of stone. To be sure, more large stone sculpture in the round must have been made during Dynasties I and II than is known today. The larger number of stelae found testifies to contemporary productivity in the field of relief sculpture. Still, although stone was used as building material in the Early Dynastic Period, the monumental buildings of that era were mainly of mud brick. This does not necessarily mean that the kings of Dynasties I and II could not have built stone superstructures for their mud brick tombs if they had wished to do so. There may have been other factors here, such as strong religious traditions, which dictated the continued use of a softer material. But it is also possible that most of these early kings could not have commanded the number of trained masons needed to build a truly vast edifice in stone. Such evidence as we presently have seems to indicate that large advances were made both in stone sculpture and relief in late Dynasty II. Throughout the Early Dynastic Period the most common objects of stone were vessels. A number of them have quite elaborate shapes, while some seem based on objects in other materials, such as basketry and metal. They also show a technical virtuosity in carving absent in the stone sculpture of their time. Stone vessels continued to be made throughout Egyptian history, but by Dynasty IV fewer of them (Cat. 13) display the elaborate shapes of earlier periods.

The first truly monumental architectural project of Dynasty III, the funerary complex of King Djoser, was built in stone in striking contrast to the architecture of the preceding age. The material used is not the only innovation. The central element of his funerary monument is a stepped pyramid, a new type of superstructure for royal tombs, which later, in Dynasty IV, was replaced by true pyramids with smooth sloping sides. Around this edifice were a number of ritual buildings all enclosed by a great wall. Some of these, like the wall, are detailed imitations in stone of contemporary structures in reed, wood, and mud brick. They were produced in a spirit of exuberant experimentation with the new medium—rather like the stone vessels, imitating pottery shapes, mentioned above. By Dynasty IV, architectural forms more appropriate to stone were evolved. However, in the light of our current knowledge of the religious needs which brought forth the specific forms of Djoser's monument or those of Dynasty IV, these features cannot totally be ascribed to aesthetics or to advances in technical skill.

Progress in craftsmanship is also visible in the statuary and relief of Dynasty III. Djoser's funerary monument was originally equipped with a number of statues and reliefs. The most famous of the former is a seated figure of the King, found sealed in a statue chamber (or *serdab*) at the base of the pyramid. The pose resembles that of the statue of King Khasekhem of late Dynasty II (Fig. 5), a work almost its equal in the skill of the carving. However, the sculpture of Djoser is larger and less squat, and is imbued with a greater feeling of power. Other sculptures, although fragmentary or unfinished, show that Djoser's artists were experimenting, embellishing architectural elements with statuary as well as with at least one group sculpture—assumed to be such from the remnants of four aligned pairs of feet.

These innovations, interestingly enough, may all have been the work of a single man, a high official of Djoser named Imhotep who in later times was famous as an architect, astronomer, priest, wise man, and physician. Eventually he was deified.

Most of the sculptures from Djoser's funerary complex are of limestone, but one Dynasty III royal head in granite demonstrates that the sculptors of the time could carve even colossal statuary in hard stone with a greater degree of modeling than that known earlier. This granite head comes from one of the relatively few over lifesize sculptures of the Old Kingdom which have been preserved. In later periods these apparently became more common. However, it must be remembered that the vast majority of Egyptian sculpture was lifesize or, in the main, smaller.

A figure of a god (Cat. 12), one of Dynasty III's small royal sculptures, shows how rapidly the artists of the day were progressing in the creation of a new style. This figure strides with its left leg forward, a pose not without precedent and closely linked to the stone statuary of later times. This type of striding, idealized, muscular figure, often with both hands held at the sides, is one of the standard sculptural types used for representations both of kings and private persons from Dynasty IV onward (Fig. 10; Cat. 24 and 25). In fact, this early sculpture of a god is already in the style of Dynasty IV, except for the rather simplified modeling of the face and the large head and torso.

Dynasty IV style is also closely anticipated in royal reliefs of Dynasty III. For example, although certain reliefs made for King Djoser display some stiffness of form and relatively squat proportions with large heads, others (Fig. 12) have more elegant proportions, close to those common later on.

Similar stylistic and technical advances can be seen in the art created for the upper classes. Their tombs now came to be provided with chapels where offerings were to be made, adorned with relief in both wood and stone. In one chapel, there were also paintings including some scenes of daily life in addition to representations of the deceased or offerings to him. Genre themes were more frequent in the tombs of the later Old Kingdom. The few known private sculptures of Dynasty III tend to have somewhat archaic proportions, being rather squat, sometimes with very large heads. They are also stiffer than most later sculptures; and most of them have one arm held across the chest, reminiscent of the statue of Khasekhem (Fig. 5) and the seated statue of Djoser, as well as of early figures both in the round and in relief. This pose became far less common in Dynasty IV when new attitudes, developed in royal sculptures, were taken over for statues of private persons.

The kings of Dynasty IV inherited from their predecessors property and power. Their artists were equipped with skills and with the basic elements of style to be used in an endeavor to record for eternity that wealth and power. These artistic resources were immediately developed and exploited to such a point that the monuments created for the rulers of early Dynasty IV are generally considered to be the most majestic statement of Egyptian kingship.

Like the rulers before them, the kings of Dynasty IV were considered as man in the role of god, as demigod, or as actual incarnation of the god. By virtue of this fact the king was not only the religious head of the country, but was also the intermediary between gods and men. The gods owned the land governed for them by the king, and it was from his hands that both spiritual and temporal blessings flowed.

Although the supreme status of the Egyptian king in this era is well expressed in the monuments of Sneferu, first pharaoh of Dynasty IV, the most impressive statement of kingship was built by his successor, Cheops: the Great Pyramid at Giza, the largest monument ever erected in Egypt.

The regal austerity and monumentality of this royal tomb finds a close sculptural counterpart in the statue of Chephren, Cheops' second successor to the throne, protected by the falcon god Horus (Fig. 3). The restrained naturalism of the king's idealized, calm face and powerful physique, combined with the unified and balanced repose of all elements of the sculpture, make this figure a perfect symbol of a being at once human and divine.

Emphasis on the simplicity and austerity of the art of Dynasty IV can be exaggerated, however. Not all the architecture was as mammoth as that of Cheops' pyramid, not all royal sculptures as majestically aloof as that of Chephren. The walls of the royal funerary temples were decorated with painted reliefs; and group sculptures of the kings and the gods (Fig. 10) as well as of the king with his queen are also known. Certainly, though, as can be seen also in the art created, often by the royal workshops, for the important officials of the day—such as the stela of Wepemnofret (Cat. 17)—a staid dignity and monumentality does pervade most of the art of the time. This tendency extends to such details as the decoration of ritual furniture (Cat. 16).

The statues of Mycerinus with various deities (Fig. 10) and another work in which he is shown striding, with his wife (carved on the same scale as he is) embracing him, are our best evidence for the development of royal group sculptures in the Old Kingdom. Prior to this time our evidence for this sort of royal statuary consists of the aligned pairs of feet from Djoser's funerary monument, mentioned above, and the lower portion of a seated statue of Radedef, Cheops' immediate successor, where a small squatting figure of his queen adjoins his leg.

With the exception of group sculptures showing the king with various gods—of which we have one example in Dynasty V —our presently available evidence indicates that these sculptures had very little specific influence on later royal art. However, royal group sculpture and other works appear to have had a profound influence on the Old Kingdom's private sculpture. The fragmentary statue of Radedef is the first example of the pose it portrays, and is probably the ultimate prototype for compositions such as Cat. 25. Similarly, a royal sculpture of the type represented by the striding pair of Mycerinus and his wife would have been the original source of striding pair statues of husbands and wives (Cat. 24). And, although our first evidence for the pose assumed by King Chephren (Fig. 3), with both hands resting on the knees, is in a private work of the time of Cheops, it may be assumed that it also originated ultimately in now lost sculptures of that king. It is the pose, known also in minor variations, most commonly assumed by seated male figures in the Old Kingdom (Cat. 21 and 23), generally replacing the more archaic pose of one arm held across the chest, found in royal and private sculptures of Dynasty III.

The art of the Old Kingdom demonstrates a unity of style greater than in later periods, partly because the private art depended so much upon contemporary royal prototypes. Many of the finest private works were actually made in the royal workshops, while others clearly show the direct influence of such works. The degree to which private art followed the patterns of royal art would have depended upon the degree to which the same forms could serve the related but nevertheless different religious and magical purposes for which royal art and private art were created.

For example, in Dynasties IV and V a limited number of highly naturalistic and individualized tomb sculptures were created for private persons. Such forms were not found in the period's royal statuary because the purpose of the latter was to convey the idea of the office of kingship more than the "flesh and blood" reality of an individual king. Similarly, while private persons might sometimes be shown with physical deformities, the king was always represented with the same perfect muscular body as the gods. Most private persons were indeed also portrayed in this manner; occasionally men other than kings could also be shown conventionally, but perhaps tending to conform somewhat more to reality—that is, represented as being middle-aged and prosperously portly (Cat. 20).

As noted earlier, several important developments occurred during Dynasty V (2450–2290 B.C.) in the society of the Old Kingdom and in its art. In the royal sphere, the most striking of these phenomena was the rise to great prominence of the cult of the sun god Re. Although only two temples dedicated to that god have been discovered (of which one is fully excavated), inscriptions indicate that at least six kings of the Dynasty built temples to Re. These temples, to judge from the one excavated, were decorated with scenes depicting royal rituals as well as representations of seasonal human and animal activities of daily life—as though to portray the all-encompassing power of the sun. Details of these daily life scenes appear both in royal funerary temples and in some private tombs, presumably with the royal reliefs as inspiration. Also noticeable in the royal temples are scenes having to do with the particular achievements of individual kings.

In the private sphere, as we have noted, there was a great increase in the number of tombs and statues, accompanied by a proliferation of tomb chapels. More and more scenes of private daily life were introduced, the compositions busier and livelier than in the preceding Dynasty. A number of motifs formerly restricted to royal monuments passed into the repertoire of private tomb decoration. In some cases in late Dynasty V and early Dynasty VI, the tombs of the most important officials expanded in size and had far larger cult chambers with more decorated wall space than in earlier times. In addition, they took on something of the character of a monument to the memory of the great owner, as well as being magical cult places to ensure the official's continued existence after death.

As time progressed, still other changes occurred. In the field of royal statuary, for example, Dynasty VI witnessed the first appearance of several new types of sculptures (Fig. 9 and Cat. 19). The style of certain of these works betrays a growing formalism in the art of the time. Although primarily nonindividualistic, the statuary and reliefs of the Old Kingdom were basically naturalistic. This naturalism continued throughout the period—indeed, it survived throughout Egyptian history. However, in late Dynasty V and in Dynasty VI one finds a number of pieces displaying stylizations which give them a somewhat less natural appearance. In part this must have been related to the general decline in the quality of most sculptures, as evidenced in their more summary modeling. This is visible even in royal works of the latter part of Dynasty V, such as Cat. 18. This piece, although continuing in the tradition of earlier works—such as the statue of Mycerinus (Fig. 10)—is stiffer and more simply modeled. In private works these stylistic features may sometimes be far more visible (Cat. 22).

But diminished technical skill alone cannot account for some stylizations which begin to appear in sculpture in the round. For example, certain statues both in stone and wood come to have facial features, such as elongated and tilted eyes, which differ from the more simple physiognomies of the larger mass of sculptures. In wooden pieces, which generally displayed much the same proportions and a greater degree of naturalism, we begin to find figures with somewhat attenuated bodies and limbs. Inasmuch as more naturalistic renderings in wood continued to be made (Cat. 26), and some of these wooden figures were skillfully carved, this change could not have been due solely to a decline in ability; it would also seem to reflect a new tendency in the art of the time.

By the end of Dynasty VI, although the country remained politically united for yet another few decades, the real power of Old Kingdom rulers had vanished with the loss of their land. This loss was caused by the breaking up of former royal estates through a growing circle of inheritance, by the large building projects undertaken, and by the great number of tax-exempt estates dedicated to the upkeep of mortuary cults. In the provinces, this weakening of the central power made it possible for a provincial nobility to arise. After the short-lived Dynasties VII and VIII (2155–2135 B.C.) the political unity of Egypt was shattered. It was not until 2040 B.C. that the country was once again united. The interval separating the collapse of the Old Kingdom and the reunification is known as the First Intermediate Period.

The end of the Old Kingdom had profound effects on an art so long nurtured by the patronage of a powerful court. In the north at Memphis, and presumably at the new center of power at Herakleopolis to the south of Memphis, the old traditions were generally maintained but with a reduction in the scale of the monuments built and a decline in technical skill manifested.

In those areas further to the south, already somewhat provincial in relation to Memphis, the art changed more dramatically. In some places the traditions of the old Memphite school of relief work were continued but with a lessening of artistic ability. In other places, although various styles coexisted, there was a change toward crude modification of the older Memphite forms. This trend was characterized, in relief, by figures with sharp edges and little or no modeling (Cat. 29), and sometimes by oddly proportioned, stiff, attenuated figures (Cat. 30 and 31). Such figures are similar to the numerous wooden tomb sculptures of the day (Cat. 28), themselves pale reflections of the finer wooden works of earlier times. One need only compare these First Intermediate Period stelae to a fine low relief of Dynasty IV (Cat. 17) or a relief in the bolder style of Dynasty V (Cat. 20a) to see how greatly the art had changed.

However, even if these later styles, which also seem to reflect the more formal tendencies entering Old Kingdom art toward the end of Dynasty V, were primarily born of a lack of craftsmanship, they do display aesthetic feelings characteristic of their time and locale. Their stylistic features became new conventions which were sometimes developed even when artists had acquired a greater degree of ability. As we shall see, these forms helped in no small way to give rise to the art of the Middle Kingdom.

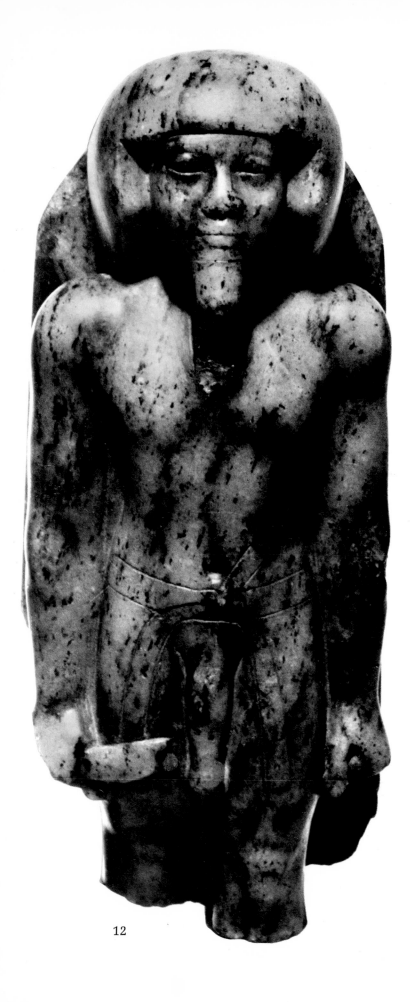

Cat. 12. Bearded deity with knife. Although it has been dated to Dynasty III because of such early features as its short neck, the relatively large size of its head and torso, and the form of its wig and back slab, this sculpture also embodies the essential features of later idealized, youthful, striding male figures. The penis sheath identifies the subject as a god such as Ha or Onuris having associations with Libya. This rare early sculpture of a god may have been enshrined in a Memphite sanctuary (such as Djoser's Step Pyramid) as one of a group of deities representing the political divisions of Egypt. Diorite. Height 21.4 cm.

12

Cat. 13. Bowl with scalloped rim. The form denies the hardness of the stone; and the Egyptian's early mastery of stoneworking may derive in part from the manufacture of such vessels. Although an alabaster bowl of similar form is known from Dynasty II, this vessel, unless it was an heirloom, dates to Dynasty IV, the time of the tomb where it was found. Diorite. Diameter 20 cm.

Cat. 14. Necklace of steatite and carnelian beads with gold amulets in the form of legs and an adze. Tentatively reconstructed by its excavators from a confused mass of beads and amulets in a tomb which, on the basis of type, contents, and position in the cemetery, was attributed to late Dynasty III, this necklace is an example of the taste and practical aspirations of the provincial middle class. Length 28.0 cm.

14

13

15a

15b

Cat. 15a. Head of a king. Wearing the crown of Upper Egypt, this sculpture comes from one of the few colossal statues preserved from the Old Kingdom. It is at the same time one of the equally rare royal sculptures of Dynasty III. Its full face and plastic modeling (best visible in Cat. 15b, a plaster cast not in the exhibition) also relate to the art of early Dynasty IV, but the shape of the crown, the simplicity of the features, and the almost sullen expression are more characteristic of Dynasty III. This head, never totally polished, may have been painted. The collar suggests a garb customarily associated with a royal ritual of rejuvenation, similar to that of Fig. 5. Red granite. Height 54.3 cm.

Cat. 16. Lion's head. The remains of a ledge with corner on the right indicates that it, like similar pieces, once decorated the right front corner of an offering or an embalming table. As its few dated stylistic parallels are works of Dynasty IV, this head is best attributed to that period. Figures of lions magically guarded many types of ritual furniture (Fig. 3) as well as temples (Cat. 11). Alabaster. Height 17.0 cm.

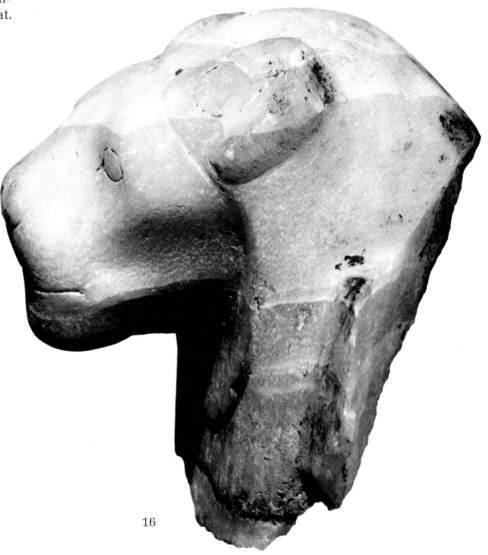

16

17

Cat. 17. Stela of Wepemnofret. Around his Great Pyramid King Cheops of Dynasty IV provided tombs for his relatives. Some of these, like Wepemnofret's, had decoration limited to a stela showing the deceased seated at a table with offerings. This stela embodies some essential features of Old Kingdom funerary beliefs and tomb decoration. Gracing a niche in the tomb chapel, it marked the place where offerings were to be made, while its representations and inscriptions might magically guarantee the deceased's enjoyment of the necessities of eternal life.

The forms, less elongated than in reliefs of Dynasty III (Fig. 12), are simple and well spaced, the composition a stately asymmetrical balance of horizontals and verticals. Low relief existed prior to the time of Cheops, but this form of extremely low relief with very subtle modeling was an innovation of his sculptors. The clear but subdued color scheme is also in keeping with Dynasty IV's royal tradition of dignity and expert craftsmanship.

Bonds between art and writing are close. Each hieroglyph is itself a detailed representation and most of the decoration is an interesting composition of inscriptions, in part made possible by the flexibility of orientation of the script and in part dictated by traditions governing that orientation. The signs before Wepemnofret's face, in the next six columns to the right, and around the table face toward him as they list offerings to him. Those in the top line and two columns farthest to the right, which list his titles, and those in his name above his head face right as does his figure. Painted limestone. Height 44.8 cm.

Cat. 18 is here identified as Nyuserre of Dynasty V because most details of its style have parallels in a sculpture inscribed for that King. But so few royal statues of Dynasty V are known that the identification must remain tentative.

Only a few royal sculptures have been preserved from Dynasty VI, and most of them are quite unlike earlier royal statuary. For example, the only Old Kingdom metal sculptures of kings are two VIth Dynasty copper figures, and the majority of the period's stone sculptures differ from royal statuary in stone of Dynasties IV and V in their smaller scale, type of representation, and style—especially in the carving of limbs free from the block of stone. The figure of Pepy II seated on his mother's lap (Cat. 19) is unique, and a figure of Pepy I made earlier in Dynasty VI is the sole Old Kingdom example of a sculptural type known from later periods: the king kneeling to present offerings. Still other sculptures of the period, such as Fig. 3, represent interesting variations on earlier themes—the king with protective falcon (Fig. 3) and the king in a garb associated with a royal ritual of rejuvenation. However, a royal inscription indicates that a copper statue was made as early as Dynasty II. And since some of the stone sculptures come from temples to the gods rather than funerary temples of kings, our main source for royal statuary of Dynasties IV and V, there is a slight possibility that similar types of figures were made earlier. But for some works there is no reason to postulate an earlier model, and such is the case for Cat. 19. This clearly expresses a temporary peculiarity in the power structure: the throne occupied by a child. In the preferred rectilinear and unemotional manner of the Old Kingdom, the king is shown, as a miniature adult in the traditional pose and garb of authority, discreetly supported by his mother.

Cat. 18. Bust from a statue of a king. This sculpture, datable to Dynasty V, portrays the king with back pillar, wearing the *nemes*-headcloth, one of the most common elements of royal regalia. Red granite. Height 34.0 cm.

18

Cat. 19. King Pepy II seated on the lap of Meryre-ankhnes. The fifth king of Dynasty VI wears the *nemes*-headcloth; his mother wears the vulture headdress of queens and goddesses. Alabaster. Height 39.2 cm.

19

20a

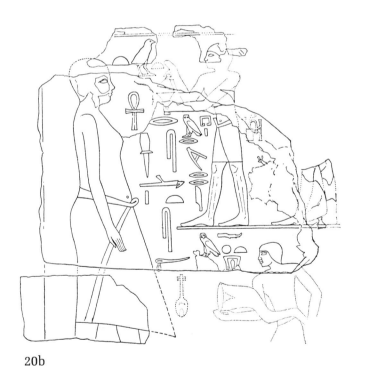

20b

Cat. 20a. Relief from the tomb of Semenkhu-Ptah Itwesh. That this figure represents a statue of Itwesh is demonstrated by the third line of text before his face, reading either "lifelike statue," which could refer to the physique and the unusual skull shape and physiognomy, or "living statue," a reference to its function. Some idea of the mature, portly type of figure shown here may be gained from Cat. 20b (not in exhibition), a reconstruction of a scene showing a similarly labeled figure receiving offerings. In both, the near shoulder is in perspective, a device perhaps more common in representations of statues of important persons than in those of the persons themselves. A statue of this type, with arm advanced to hold a staff, would have been of wood. Inscriptions from Itwesh's tomb place the relief in late Dynasty V, a date which well suits its bold style. Limestone. Height 42.6 cm.

Cat. 21. Seated statue of a man named Kathesu. The body is painted reddish brown, the kilt and eyeballs white, the collar yellow. The pupils, eyebrows, wig, and simple cubic seat were black. Late Dynasty V. From same tomb as Cat. 22. Limestone. Height 36.0 cm.

Cat. 22. Standing statue of a woman named Ithetka. Body and back slab are painted yellow, the collar red and black. The base, the space between arms and body, eyebrows, and details of the eyes are black. Late Dynasty V. From the same tomb as Cat. 21. Limestone. Height 40.0 cm.

Tomb sculptures proliferated in type and quantity in Dynasties IV and V. Cat. 21-24 are in many ways representative of the sculptures of the latter period. Although seated, standing, and striding figures were made earlier, the royal works of Dynasty IV are the ultimate prototypes of the poses of Hetepy and Kathesu (Cat. 21 and 23) and probably for the type of the striding pair (Cat. 24). Family groups are most common in the Old Kingdom. Also of that time are the round, open faces and the relatively simple wigs and garments. Youthful bodies predominate in all periods as does the convention of reddish brown for men's skins and yellow for women's, reflecting the male's more frequent exposure to the sun.

21

22

23

Cat. 23. Seated pair statue of a man named Hetepy and his wife Renpetnefret. Hetepy wears a short kilt and wig. Renpetnefret, who embraces him, wears a tight v-neck dress with shoulder straps. Late Dynasty IV or early Dynasty V. Limestone. Height 42.0 cm.

Cat. 24. Statue of a husband and wife. He strides forward from a back slab cut to the contour of his head and shoulder. She, adorned with anklets, bracelets, collar, and neck band, stands embracing him. Second half of Dynasty V. Limestone. Height 73.0 cm.

24

Cat. 25. Statue of a man with his wife and son. Datable to the second half of Dynasty V, this sculpture may have belonged to a man named Iruka-Ptah. Because its figures are carved on different scales the sculpture seems more a symbolic expression of ranking and relationships than a representation of an actual family. The large figure of the husband strides forward, his wife and son attached to him by gestures of affection and dependence. A parallel for the pose of the woman exists in a royal sculpture of Dynasty IV and, less close, a relief of King Djoser of Dynasty III. Somewhat similar family groupings occur in Dynasty V private reliefs. Limestone. Height 73.5 cm.

25

Cat. 26a. Figure of a boy. Although its large head and plump body constitute an unusual attempt to render more naturalistically a child's body, the figure is a type (Cat. 25) —nude, with sidelock, finger held to mouth—signifying "boy." Cat. 26b (not in exhibition) shows the piece as it was found next to a sarcophagus in a burial chamber. Second half of Dynasty V. Wood. Height 44.0 cm.

26a

26b

27

Cat. 27. Woman grinding grain.
Starting in Dynasty IV, servants figures were placed in tombs to serve
the deceased. Unlike sculptures of
their owners, such figures are
shown in active poses. Their non-
idealized faces and bodies may be
realistic to the point of caricature.
Dynasty V or VI. Limestone.
Height 18.5 cm.

Cat. 28. Standing nude woman.
Sculptures of this type were made
from the late Old Kingdom into the
Middle Kingdom. Like many other
contemporary wooden sculptures,
some have elongated limbs and
bodies. Found in tombs, often in
quantity, their purpose is uncertain. Like Cat. 1, 45, and 46, they
have sometimes been interpreted
as concubines. Probably First Intermediate Period. Wood. Height
40.5 cm.

28

29

30

Cat. 29. Saby receiving offerings. Cut off from the old royal centers of art in the North, the southern provincial artists of this politically unsettled era developed styles which, as this stela demonstrates, display less technical skill and are less orthodox in composition and color, but which sometimes have a greater liveliness than their Old Kingdom ancestors. First Intermediate Period. Limestone. Height 43.6 cm.

Cat. 30. Funerary stela. Inscribed for the official Inheret-nakht and his wife Benit, priestess of the goddess Hathor. Shown before a pile of offerings, the two figures are carved in a local Upper Egyptian style characterized by angular, high-waisted figures with large, pointed noses. Late First Intermediate Period. Limestone. Height 65.0 cm.

Cat. 31. Funerary stela of a priestess of Hathor. Setnet-Inheret, for whose eternal benefit her husband dedicated this monument, stands holding a mirror. Mirrors (Cat. 72), in addition to having some association with Hathor, may have been believed to have revitalizing powers for the deceased. The offerings floating in space, the crudely carved and unevenly spaced hieroglyphs, the elongated body, large eyes, and thick lips testify to a southern provincial origin in the First Intermediate Period or early Middle Kingdom. Limestone. Height 65.2 cm.

31

III. The Middle Kingdom

The history of the First Intermediate Period, preceding the Middle Kingdom, is that of the long struggle between the kings of Dynasties IX and X (ca. 2134–2040 B.C.) at Herakleopolis and the early Dynasty XI (2134–1991 B.C.) kings of Thebes. With the passage of time the territory controlled by Thebes expanded and its strength grew to the point where one of the Thebian kings, Nebhepetre Mentuhotep II, overcame the last resistance of the Herakleopolitans and their supporters among the provincial nobility and reunited the country. This momentous event, about 2040 B.C., ushered in the period we call the Middle Kingdom (Dynasties XI and XII, 2040–1785 B.C.) and parts of Dynasty XIII (1785–1715 B.C.).

The reunification of Egypt did not, however, restore the political unity it had known throughout the Old Kingdom. Neither Mentuhotep II nor his successors, Mentuhotep III and IV, were in a position to suppress totally the feudal nobility. Furthermore, when Amenemhat I, first king of Dynasty XII (1991–1785 B.C.) usurped the throne, not only was that event accompanied by internal disorder but he restored many of their ancient privileges to the nobility which had helped him gain the kingship. In fact, it was not until much further on in Dynasty XII, late in the reign of King Sesostris III, that the political power of these lords of Middle and Upper Egypt was crushed and the kingship of Egypt restored to a real semblance of its former might.

The consolidation of power in the hands of Sesostris II and his successor, Amenemhat III, enabled them to make marked progress in certain projects begun by former rulers: the domination of Nubia and the reclamation of large tracts of land from the lake in the Fayoum, the oasis to the west of the Nile Valley south of Memphis. This is not to say that the pharaohs of the Middle Kingdom prior to Sesostris were weak or ineffectual;

most of them enjoyed prosperous reigns and a great degree of power. On the other hand, neither they nor their mightier followers could recapture the full royal glory of the Old Kingdom.

The collapse of the central power after Dynasty VIII and the disruption of the country by wars between rival kings dependent upon the support of powerful provicincial nobles could not help but deprive the kingship of some of the divine status it had enjoyed in an older, more secure era. Like their predecessors, the rulers of the Middle Kingdom were officially more than human; numerous texts equate them with various deities and portray them as equal partners with the gods. However, there are also inscriptions which place a new stress on their royal individuality and personal achievement and represent the kings less as infallible deities than as supermen, liable to error, charged by the gods with the task of governing the land so as to cause both it and its people to prosper.

These new concepts find their finest artistic expression in the statuary of Kings Sesostris III and Amenemhat III. The former was the first ruler of Egypt to have his face represented in a realistic fashion. Sometimes his facial features have a careworn, almost melancholy expression. In other works, although they also have heavy-lidded eyes and down-turned mouth, the King appears stronger and more determined (Cat. 40a-b). It is worth noting, however, that his body shows nothing of such realism but rather retains both the regal pose and ideal, muscular physique traditional for statues of kings since Dynasty IV (Fig. 3). If the pharaoh had become occasionally more human, he had not altogether stepped down from his divine throne.

The First Intermediate Period had brought other important cultural changes which in turn had a profound effect upon the art. While private persons in the Old Kingdom might as delegates of the king serve the gods as priests and priestesses, there is, in connection with their afterlife, little reference to deities except to indicate that eternal life was a gift from the king and the gods. The pharaoh in his pyramid might expect to be transformed into a god after death, indeed to be equated with various deities; but private persons seemed more closely bound to an existence intimately associated with the tomb, more or less resembling life on earth. These ideas did not vanish, but new ideas sprung up alongside them.

With the decline and fall of the Old Kingdom the funerary rites and rituals, once the prerogative of the pharoah, were adopted by private persons who could thus aspire to a more elevated existence in the hereafter. At first this "democratization" of the hereafter was more or less limited to the powerful nobles and primarily associated with the version of life in the hereafter ruled over by the sun god. Gradually, however, all Egyptians who could secure the proper funerary equipment, such as coffins inscribed with the necessary magic spells, could look forward to expanded possibilities of eternal life. And not only were formerly royal magic spells taken over; powerful royal symbols such as crowns and scepters came to be represented as possessions of the deceased on the sides of coffins of private persons. Another regal or perhaps even divine attribute such as the *uraeus* (Cat. 43) appeared on the private jewelry of the time. Most important, however, Osiris became the main god of the dead. From this point on the deceased honored by, justified by, and (though until after the Middle Kingdom, only rarely) identified with Osiris could hope to share in the bounty of that great god.

These religious changes became manifest not only in the decoration of coffins and jewelry but also in relief and the statuary. Elaborate tombs were still carved; their decoration, as well as the statuary made for them, remained of magical importance for the deceased. However, unlike the Old Kingdom during which private statuary and stelae had only been made for the tombs, both private statues and stelae were now made to be placed in sacred precincts, especially that of Osiris at Abydos, where they might enable their deceased owners to participate magically in the religious ceremonies in his honor and share in the bounty of the royal offerings to him. More visible than in former days, the statuary now was meant to be seen and to have its inscriptions read by priests and other pious visitors. Sculptures were sometimes inserted in niches in stelae. Many of them, including family groups, really became stelae with figures carved half in the round against the stone slab; and both the slab and the figures' garments were decorated with inscriptions. An interesting variation on this theme is displayed by Cat. 41. The artist, faced with the task of representing a man wrapped in a heavy robe—together with a woman, probably his wife—has solved the problem by carving her half in the round against the front of the man's robe and neatly framed with an inscription.

Because they were exposed to the elements and to human touch, the sculptures were increasingly made of hard stone. Unlike the limestone tomb sculptures of the Old Kingdom, the Middle Kingdom stone was probably generally left unpainted. The nature of the material and the need to decorate the figures with inscriptions would appear to have led to a preference for figures of simple form wrapped in heavy robes or wearing long skirts suitable as fields for decoration. However, these stylistic trends should probably also be viewed as expressing religious beliefs as well as the general spirit of the time. The cult of Osiris quite possibly was directly responsible for the creation of one sculptural form—the block statue (Cat. 41). At any rate, the general spiritual tenor of the times, its beliefs and practices, and its dominant aesthetic sensibilities favored the production of isolated, individual figures with more somber expressions than the somewhat cheerful family groups of the Old Kingdom.

Not all these changes in the art of the Middle Kingdom took place immediately. In fact, many did not occur until rather late in Dynasty XII. Before then, there were other interesting developments.

As it was a Southern Egyptian Dynasty which united the two lands, it is hardly surprising that the early manifestations of its art are in a style dependent upon that of Upper and Middle Egypt in the First Intermediate Period. It seems reasonable to suppose that as the power of Thebes grew, even prior to the reunification of Egypt, the better artists of the day would have been attracted to a court already undertaking the construction of important monuments, and that a royal style would therefore evolve. This in fact is what we are confronted with in the preserved monuments of the period.

Before Mentuhotep II united the country he had begun work on a large funerary monument at the foot of the bay in the Theban mountains now known as Deir el Bahri. Along with his own burial place, he constructed a tomb there for his chief Queen, Neferu. The style of the relief decoration in Neferu's tomb (Cat. 32 and 33a-b) is in most respects typical for the early part of Mentuhotep's reign—characterized by tall, high-waisted figures with long necks and by severe contours with little modulation. Equally striking is the fact that the facial features are applied to the head as individual entities rather than modeled or integrated into a standard facial structure. The eyes are elongated, with exaggerated tear ducts, and are outlined with thick paint stripes. The noses are rather blunt; the lips, set close to the nose, are thick. The ears are highly stylized with flattened lobes. Mannered too in appearance are the hands, which indicate the actions represented but do not perform them in a naturalistic fashion. This is, however, not unusual in Egyptian art where the allusion to a gesture intended is often more important than its naturalistic representation.

Certain contemporary reliefs, both sunk and raised, show a minute attention to the depiction of details of wig, jewelry, and garments, but in other respects are quite alike. A comparison of Neferu's reliefs with Cat. 30 and, more striking, Cat. 31, should clearly indicate the southern origins of this style. A comparison of these same reliefs with Cat. 17 or 20 will demonstrate how far they differ from the Memphite norms of the Old Kingdom.

Following the reunification and the attendant increased contact between South and North, the severe southern style came to be modified, but not submerged, by the more naturalistic Memphite art of the Old Kingdom. This is seen in the sculpture created for Mentuhotep II after his conquest of the North. Some of the reliefs of that time (Cat. 34) are only slightly different from those created earlier in his reign, while others make it clear that an attempt was being made to regain the artistic glory of what was considered a golden age.

The influence of that former age is more pronounced in the proportions and elegant, modulated contours of another Southern Egyptian relief, this one made in the time of Mentuhotep III (Cat. 35). Sharing specific details of garb and style with reliefs in the funerary temple of Pepy II of Dynasty VI at Saqqara, it appears to indicate a deliberate seeking of inspiration in the royal monuments of the past. However, the facial features, crisp outline, and rendering of minute details also link this XIth Dynasty piece to other reliefs in the South. In Dynasty XII archaizing tendencies in the art are even more pronounced. Although its kings were of southern origin and built many monuments in the South, they shifted the capital to a more central location, founding a new one just south of Memphis. Nearby, a royal cemetery was begun at a site now called Lisht. There the funerary complexes of the Dynasty's first two kings, Amenemhat I and Sesostris I, and a number of private tombs show clear links to the Memphite Old Kingdom monuments.

For example, the relief of a gooseherd from a private tomb (Cat. 37) was certainly copied from a relief, royal or private, of Dynasty VI. It was in that period that servants first were shown in precisely this pose. The elegant curve of the birds' bodies and wings, the subtle modeling of the figures and modulation of contours also link this relief to Old Kingdom art. However, the fact that the relief is relatively low may relate it more to reliefs prior to late Dynasty V. This is perhaps not accidental, for certain monuments of the kings of the early Old Kingdom not only served as inspirations for reliefs of Amenemhat I, they were incorporated into his own pyramid as rubble fill. Amenemhat's use of his predecessors' monuments as quarries need not be considered a sacrilege or indicative of disrespect. The temples may already have fallen into ruin and their funerary cults abandoned. There is evidence that a king's obligations to the cult of his forebears did not necsesarily entail the preservation of their monuments. It also seems probable that such reusing of stones served several positive functions: the expression of the continuity of kingship, the bringing of the old monuments to new life, the magical linking of a king with those who came before him. Perhaps of importance to a new dynasty wishing to achieve a greater aura of legitimacy, there may have been in this a propagandistic purpose as well—supported by contemporary literary propaganda in the form of inscriptions.

The monuments created for Sesostris I at Lisht were also archaizing and, as in the case of the monuments of Dynasty XI, the model chosen was the funerary complex of King Pepy II of Dynasty VI. This was the last great royal monument of the Old Kingdom, and its builder's cult was still important in the Middle Kingdom. The plan of Sesostris I's funerary temple was closely based on that of Pepy II; many of its reliefs were directly inspired by those adorning the older monument's walls. Although not an exact copy, the relief of the goddess Seshat (Cat. 36a) probably belonged to a scene which was certainly inspired by an Old Kingdom relief; its prototype may have been one of the representations of Pepy II smiting Egypt's enemies (Cat. 36b).

The few preserved royal reliefs of the later Middle Kingdom show various blendings of styles. To judge from the limited material we have, there was a tendency toward more schematic composition and a greater use of symbols than in the Old Kingdom.

Similar mixtures of styles are found in the series of large tombs of the nobles of Middle Egypt which were made well into the reign of Sesostris III. The decoration of these tombs retained closer connections with the art of the North than the areas further to the south. In these tombs we also find, possibly because they were not bound by the purposes of royal art, some experimentation in the use of perspective, certain attempts to unify large compositions not divided into registers, and an increased commemoration of specific events.

In the numerous private stelae we can see the elimination of the more severe stylizations (Cat. 42). As was characteristic of Upper Egypt in the First Intermediate Period, as time passed greater use was made of symbols and of figures of the gods. But, with the exception of one relief, it is only in sculpture in the round that we can observe the most striking development in the art of the Middle Kingdom: the introduction, in the reign of Sesostris III, of more realistically rendered faces.

The statuary of the early Middle Kingdom shows an evolution similar to that of the reliefs: a blending of regional styles, the continuation of old types, and the development of new ones. Cat. 38, for example, made early in Dynasty XII, has a broad, open face, indebted to Memphite art of the Old Kingdom. With the large ears pushed forward by the massive wig, it also has a heavier appearance, in keeping with the spirit of its age. A far more sophisticated and monumental blending of styles is visible in the head of a princess or queen from a sphinx of mid-Dynasty XII (Cat. 39). With a more sober and determined expression, its size and strength could hardly have failed to impress the viewer with the power of royalty.

Under Sesostris III and Amenemhat III the realistic depiction of the royal physiognomies came to influence private statuary. This of course was usual in Egypt, where royal works generally established the country's artistic norms. Sometimes the private sculptors produced fairly faithful copies of the royal works; sometimes they even accentuated the determined or careworn expressions of the royal sculptures. In other cases, such as Cat. 41, the influence was limited to a more realistic rendering of the face than in former times, with facial features such as eyes and lips similar to those of the royal works, but not mirroring them. The simple, though subtly modeled forms of the block are in sharp contrast to the face. However, this is merely a pronounced statement of a general tendency in Egyptian sculpture, where the body, important as a symbol, including the gestures it makes, is generally less individualistic and often more summarily modeled than the face.

Fine and often innovative works continued to be made into Dynasty XIII; often it is difficult to distinguish between these pieces and those of late Dynasty XII. However, the country again lost its political unity midway in Dynasty XIII (1785–1650 B.C.), which started the Second Intermediate Period (Dynasties XIII–XVII, ca. 1715 to ca. 1551 B.C.) and brought about a decline in the arts—although not as severe a decline as in the First Intermediate Period—followed by a revival in the next era.

Before passing from the Middle Kingdom, however, a word should be said about its minor arts—which, as do the major pieces, manifest distinct links with the period following.

Middle Kingdom royal jewelry is renowned for its craftsmanship and beauty, and this is reflected in private works such as an intricate gold *uraeus* (Cat. 43). In jewelry as well as in other arts there is also evident—for example in the appearance of spiral patterns (Cat. 43 and 44)—increased artistic contact with the Near East and the Aegean. Nor was this influence one-sided. Excavations at several sites, such as at Byblos on the coast of Lebanon, have produced large numbers of Egyptianizing objects.

What historians now call Dynasty XIII (1785–1650 B.C.) was a series of kings of various origins, many of whom ruled only for a few years, but in their short reigns were able to undertake important royal building projects, though on reduced scales in comparison to those of Dynasty XII. Additions were made to temples, the relief decoration conforming more or less to the norms established during the previous dynasty. Statues, even colossal sculptures, were still being produced; and some of the period's creations, especially private works, continued to display essentially the same type of realistic features first developed in the sculptures of Sesostris III (Cat. 40) and Amenemhat III of Dynasty XII. However, after Amenemhat III, the physiognomies of the royal sculptures—and the same is true of private statuary—gradually became more idealized, the faces less lined and careworn.

As the reconstruction (Cat. 33b, not in exhibition) indicates, these fragments in sunk relief come from a hairdressing scene in the tomb of Queen Neferu of Dynasty XI. Henut has pinned up one lock and is working on another . Inu holds a third lock in readiness for insertion into the Queen's wig. The elongated, angular figures; manneristic hands; fussy detail; treatment of facial features as separate entities set into the head; the long eyes with wide paint stripes; thick, outlined lips; and the long ears with disk-shaped lobes are features of much of the art made for King Mentuhotep II before he reunited Upper and Lower Egypt. They grow out of Upper Egyptian art of the First Intermediate Period, as a comparison with Cat. 31 partially demonstrates. Hairdressing scenes, known from the walls of both coffins and tombs, possessed some as yet unclear religious significance.

Cat. 32. The hairdresser Inu. Limestone. Height 13.2 cm.

Cat. 33a. Queen Neferu, wife of King Mentuhotep II, and the hairdresser Henut. Limestone. Height 19.0 cm.

32

33a

33b

Cat. 34. Raised relief of King Mentuhotep II. Above a frieze of hieroglyphs, including those signifying authority (was) and stability (djed), the King, with protective falcon, faces a goddess who, stated to be giving life, propels a sign of life (ankh) toward him with her staff of authority (was). Behind the King is a god who has "given (him) all joy . . . and life." To the right is part of a scene wherein a female figure, perhaps a goddess, offers cloth to a now missing figure, possibly the King. This relief is closer than Cat. 32 and 33a to the style of Old Kingdom reliefs of the North —because of increased contact between North and South after Egypt's reunification. The rendering of facial features demonstrates a continuity with the earlier less naturalistic Southern style of the reign of Mentuhotep II. Dynasty XI. Limestone. Height 75.6 cm.

Cat. 35. Raised relief of King Mentuhotep III. To the left, under the Horus falcon, the King performs a ritual dance, as in Fig. 12. To the right he faces the goddess Iunyt. She is said to have given him all authority (was) and holds a was-staff in a manner suggestive of that action. Above, Mentuhotep's Horus name (Fig. 2) receives was from a cobra, the name (or representation) of the goddess Buto. The influence of Old Kingdom art hinted at in the representation of Mentuhotep II (Cat. 34) is here in the following reign clearly stronger, as evidenced by the more natural proportions, more elegant drawings, and subtle modeling. Dynasty XI. Limestone. Height 80.1 cm.

34

35

36a

Cat. 36a. Sunk relief of Seshat, goddess of writing. This piece was found in the Dynasty XII funerary temple of King Sesostris I at Lisht, where the goddess, papyrus and brush in hand, was shown recording the victory of the king over Egypt's traditional enemies. A good idea of the appearance of this large scene may be gained from the reconstruction of a similar scene in the temple of King Pepy II of Dynasty VI (Cat. 36b, not in exhibition). Although the scenes were not identical, there is a relationship between them. While Sesostris I's Dynasty XII version was executed in sunk relief, a technique not used for large scale wall decoration in Old Kingdom temples, it is based at least in part on an Old Kingdom prototype; and Sesostris' temple plan and decoration were influenced by the funerary temple of Pepy II. Limestone. Height 52.5 cm.

36b

Cat. 37. An offering of fowl for the deceased. From a private tomb of early Dynasty XII, this raised relief, with its elegant sweeping lines and meticulous modeling, is based on a Dynasty VI representation of a procession of servants, each with birds in hand and in cages. Limestone. Height 45.8 cm.

Cat. 38. Bust from a statue of a woman. An early XIIth Dynasty variant of an Old Kingdom type with idealized, open facial features, made prior to the change in physiognomy introduced in the sculpture of Sesostris III (Cat. 40). Black mottled granite. Height 23.6 cm.

37

38

39

Cat. 39. Over life-size head of a
princess. The slant of neck and pig-
tail prove this head came from a
sphinx, and its style indicates an
attribution to the reign of Amenemhat II in mid-Dynasty XII. In
1771 it was in the hands of Gavin
Hamilton in Rome, and there is
some reason to believe it came
from Hadrian's villa at Tivoli. Gods,
kings, queens, and (mostly during
the Middle Kingdom) princesses
were shown in the guise of the
sphinx, figures of which normally
guarded sacred precincts. Dark
green stone. Height 38.9 cm.

Cat. 40a-b. Statue of King Sesostris III. Most features of this sculpture continue traditions ancient even in Dynasty XII. Statues of kings with idealized, youthful bodies, with hands in the same pose, clad in pleated kilts and *nemes*-headcloth with uraeus (Cat. 43), and seated on a low-backed throne are known as early as Dynasty IV. Some of the figure's attributes have earlier royal associations. The nine bows under Sesostris' feet, for example, represent Egypt's enemies who were similarly symbolized as defeated in Dynasty III. The bull's tail which appears between his legs (Cat. 34) had been a symbol of the king's power since Dynasty I. The facial type, however, is an innovation expressing an altered concept of kingship. While retaining some of the majestic aloofness of earlier royal images, with its heavy-lidded eyes and down-turned mouth it nevertheless gives more the impression of a real person. Black granite. Height 54.5 cm.

40a

40b

Cat. 41. Statue of Senwosret–sene-befny. Block statues, in which a man is shown seated with knees drawn up, wrapped in a heavy robe, first appear in Dynasty XII. They perhaps derive from somewhat similar wooden figures on wooden boats of Dynasty XI; and it has been argued that they represent the rebirth of the deceased, revivified by the rays of the sun, assimilated to Osiris at the moment his head emerges from a mound in the Netherworld. The small figure of a woman reminds one of Cat. 25, but here, set into the doorlike frame of inscription, no gesture connects her to the man. Isolation of figures is common in Dynasty XII group sculptures, which often have a stelalike appearance. The physiognomy of this figure of Senwosret–senebefny (made during Dynasty XII under Sesostris III or later) is partially based on that of sculptures of Sesostris III or one of his successors. The statue has been in the collections of the Empress Josephine, the Comte de Pourtalès-Gorgier, Lord Amherst, and William Randolph Hearst. Brown quartzite. Height 68.3 cm.

Cat. 42. Funerary stela inscribed for Ankhy and Neferhotep. The texts are divided and oriented symmetrically into two halves, each with prayers for one man. In the panel above the representation of a door, through which the spirit could pass, is a traditional figure seated at a table (Cat. 17). Behind him a smaller figure makes a respectful gesture. The eyes are symbols of physical prosperity and could also enable the deceased to see. From the Middle Kingdom on, private stelae, in addition to their use in tombs, came to be placed in sacred precincts to enable the deceased to benefit from the god's presence and offerings to him. Dynasty XII. Limestone. Height 59.5 cm.

41

42

43

44

Cat. 43. Uraeus. This highly stylized cobra, a goddess normally
perched protectively on the head of
royalty and deities (Cat. 40), is a
fine example both of private jewelry
of the Middle Kingdom and of the
extension of certain royal preroga-
tives to private funerary practices
after the Old Kingdom. Gold.
Height 6.4 cm.

Cat. 44. Pendant in the form of a
dog or jackal. The creature is probably the funerary god Anubis,
represented on later pectorals recumbent atop a shrine. The form of
the spirals suggests a Middle Kingdom date. Electrum (?). Height 2.2
cm.

Cat. 45 is attributed to the Middle Kingdom on the basis of dated parallels. Cat. 46 was probably made during the early New Kingdom but represents a type of figure also known from the Middle Kingdom and Second Intermediate Period. Vastly different in style, the two sculptures may have served a similar purpose. They have been interpreted as relating to the procreative powers of the deceased, as fertility goddesses, sometimes associated with Hathor, and as concubines—with the leglessness of figures such as Cat. 45 seen as a deliberate obstacle to their escape from the eternal harem. On the other hand, their discovery in the burials of women and girls as well as men, has led to their being labeled maidservants and dolls.

Cat. 45. Figure of a tattooed woman. Blue green glazed faience with black details. Height 13.1 cm.

Cat. 46. Female figure. Pottery. Height 14.5 cm.

46

45

IV. The Second Intermediate Period, the New Kingdom, and the Third Intermediate Period

B y about 1715 B.C. the power of Dynasty XIII had declined to the point where a number of rival claimants to the throne could rise to the rank of independent rulers in the Delta, which ushered in what we now call the Second Intermediate Period. These petty kings are counted as Dynasty XIV (1715–1650 B.C.). In the South the power of the kings of Dynasty XIII, ruling from the old Dynasty XII capital south of Memphis, also waned. Soon thereafter a more dramatic decline ensued in the art of that region.

This is also true of the immediately succeeding period when Dynasties XIII and XIV were replaced by the Hyksos kings of Dynasty XV (1650–1540 B.C.) and the rulers of Dynasty XVI (1650–1550 B.C.). The word Hyksos comes from the ancient Egyptian *Heka Khasut*, "rulers of foreign lands." These kings arose either from the western Asiatic population which had been building up in the Delta since late Dynasty XII or from newly arrived groups from the same region, or both. The Hyksos kings were to some extent Egyptianized, but the monuments created for and under them, to judge from the presently available evidence, consisted of minor art objects in an Egyptianizing rather than Egyptian style. This is not altogether surprising, for recent excavations near or at the Hyksos seat of power have demonstrated that part of the population of the northeastern Delta at this time had a non-Egyptian material culture similar to that of contemporary Syria-Palestine. To trace the development of Egyptian art during this period one must look to the South. There, as during the First Intermediate Period, a strong political power developed at Thebes. The Theban kings known as Dynasty XVII (1650–1550 B.C.) did not initially control the entire southern part of the country, and the extent to which they were dominated by the Hyksos is still uncertain. However, they appear to have extended rapidly their dominion over the neighboring local dynasts. About 1575 B.C. these Theban kings began a drive which, by the end of the Dynasty, succeeded in freeing most of Middle and Upper Egypt from the power of the Hyksos; they also began the reconquest of Nubia.

The kings of Dynasty XVII did not create truly monumental building projects, nor maintain the artistic standards of the Middle Kingdom. Some of the works made for these rulers have a distinctly provincial character. However, unlike the situation at the end of the Old Kingdom, southern Egypt did not enter the Second Intermediate Period as an artistic backwater. Like their Dynasty XIII predecessors, Dynasty XVII sculptors were able to produce some temple reliefs in a Middle Kingdom style.

It was Ahmose, a younger brother of the last king of Dynasty XVII, who carried the battle of liberation northward. He crushed the Hyksos power in the Delta, reunited the country, and even marched into Palestine to secure Egypt's borders. Ahmose was traditionally considered the founder of Dynasty XVIII; his accomplishments on the field of battle ended the Second Intermediate Period and ushered in the New Kingdom: Dynasties XVIII (1550–1305 B.C.), XIX (1305–1196 B.C.), and XX (1195–1080 B.C.).

Hyksos rule and the fight for independence from it had a profound effect on Egypt. The country had never in the past been totally isolated from its Near Eastern neighbors; in fact, it had been an influential power in those parts of Syria and Palestine which were important for Egypt economically. Now, however, Egypt emerged for the first time as a military nation. Most of the rulers of the first half of Dynasty XVIII devoted a good deal of their time and effort consolidating control over Nubia as well as establishing a profitable sphere of influence in the Near East. They instituted a reorganization of the country's administration, often filling key offices with comrades in arms who had distinguished themselves on the field of battle. As Egypt's material well-being grew, the arts flourished, the most noticeable change being a growing propensity toward the more elegant and sophisticated. This tendency manifests itself from the very beginning of the New Kingdom. It coexists and blends, however, with more conservative artistic tendencies, especially in the earlier years of Dynasty XVIII.

The arts of the Second Intermediate Period and early New Kingdom basically continued the traditions of art of the later Middle Kingdom. In minor arts this is well illustrated by an object such as Cat. 46, a pottery figure of a type made from

Dynasty XII on into Dynasty XVIII. The continuation of Middle Kingdom style can also be seen in Cat. 47, a more elegant version of a dagger type first known in Dynasty XII. However, starting in early Dynasty XVIII some monuments indicate not only that later Middle Kingdom elements were still a vital part of the art but that a deliberate attempt was being made to imitate the art of the earlier Middle Kingdom, specifically that of late Dynasty XI and early Dynasty XII. This trend resulted from a desire to restore to Thebes, and to gain for the new rulers of the XVIIIth Dynasty, the glory of the past still visible in the monuments of that earlier age. The copying of Middle Kingdom style was also probably part of a conscious desire of the rulers of a new Theban dynasty to express a kinship with their great Theban predecessors who had similarly reunited a divided Egypt. Such a tendency is evident in the representation (Cat. 48) of Amenhotep I, second king of Dynasty XVIII, which, in its bold relief and facial features, is close in style to reliefs of King Sesostris I of Dynasty XII at Karnak. While some of the reliefs of Amenhotep I have facial features based on those of the Middle Kingdom, others display physiognomies which shortly came to dominate royal art: smaller eyes and mouths, more fully integrated into the structure of the face; arched eyebrows; more aquiline noses. Such elements were developed in the art of Hatshepsut and Tuthmosis III, and are clearly reflected in contemporary private works, for example a sculpture of Senenmut (Cat. 54). This statue, unlike the more or less contemporary sculpture of Ahmose (Cat. 49), shows few if any real links to the art of the Middle Kingdom other than those general elements of style common to most Egyptian art. Senenmut's calm, open face, with somewhat light and elegant features, would seem out of place either in the early Middle Kingdom, when statuary generally reflected the severe stylizations of contemporary reliefs (Cat. 32 and 33a), or in the later Middle Kingdom, when many sculptures took on a more realistic, introspective, or somber appearance (Cat. 40 and 41). Although the hooked nose may represent an element of Senenmut's actual physiognomy, the face, like the faces and bodies of contemporary royal sculptures, is idealizing.

These facial features, and the statues' calm, sometimes almost benign expressions are quite in keeping with the optimistic spirit of an age born of wars of liberation followed by rapid rise to national wealth and power. This style is also appropriate to the purpose for which many of these sculptures were created; a great many of them were extremely large and imposing and made to be placed into monumental architectural settings.

The preference for relatively simple forms continued in the royal statuary of Tuthmosis III's successor, Amenhotep II, although within the reign of a given king there is a certain variety in facial features (Cat. 55). Thereafter, as expressive of a society which had achieved great cultural refinement, art became more sophisticated and complex.

The rulers of the New Kingdom enjoyed an official or godlike status which found expression in sculptures depicting them nobly enthroned or majestically striding forward in poses which had been traditional since Dynasty IV (Figs. 3 and 10). However, unlike their predecessors, these present a more human appearance, even in the role of gods.

This is reflected in greater variety of royal poses both in statuary and relief. Far more often than in the past rulers are represented carrying out their obligations to the gods by, for example, kneeling or prostrating themselves to present offerings. It is also reflected, in the temple iconography, by greater emphasis on scenes which, even if traditional, stress the actual accomplishments of kings. For example, the theme of a king smiting Egypt's enemies (Cat. 36b) had been traditional since its appearance in the tomb painting of a Predynastic king at Hierakonpolis. With Tuthmosis III, such scenes were executed on monumental scale to decorate the large gateways of temples. Similarly, although fragments of relief from both the Old and Middle Kingdoms demonstrate that actual scenes of battle were represented in temples of those periods, it is clear that they were not on the scale of those that decorated New Kingdom temples (Fig. 4 and Cat. 76). Most evidence for these scenes in the New Kingdom dates from Dynasties XIX and XX, but there are fragments preserved from the first half of Dynasty XVIII to show that such representations had become more frequent.

Recent excavations have shown that Queen Hatshepsut, who at one time was coregent with her nephew Tuthmosis III, was not as peaceable as she was once thought to be although she left no monuments portraying her as a mighty warrior. Even if in her time a traditional style remained strong, the monuments she left also reflect the novelties introduced in Dynasty XVIII.

The famous funerary temple of Hatshepsut at Deir el Bahri and the building projects she commanded for the god Amun at Karnak were the first monumental works of architecture undertaken at Thebes during the New Kingdom. In size alone, they herald the grandiose scale of things to come. Some of the reliefs in her funerary temple, such as the representations of the transportation of obelisks for the temple of Amun at Karnak and the trading expedition sent to the land of Punt, somewhere on the Red Sea coast of Africa, indicate not only Hatshepsut's devotion to the god Amun, but also her pride in her own achievements for him. Furthermore, these reliefs show a new propensity for large scale wall decoration in which detailed visual accounts are given of events, and in which landscape elements give the reliefs a hitherto unknown appearance of reality.

Similar changes occur in the private reliefs of the time. With Hatshepsut and Tuthmosis III the Theban cemeteries became the major burial ground for the high officials of the day. In their tombs, alongside older scenes showing them as the noble dead receiving offerings, watching the activities of their servants, or engaging in pastimes such as fishing and hunting, there now appeared new elements depicting these functionaries engaged in their official duties.

In the Middle Kingdom changes in religious beliefs and practices had given rise to certain new types of private sculpture, such as the block statue (Cat. 41), intimately related to the creation of a new field of private art: statuary to be placed in temples. The block statue becomes more frequent in the New Kingdom and succeeding periods. Other sculptural types, such as seated figures wrapped in heavy robes (Cat. 49), did not vanish, but were made in fewer numbers and seem a bit out of place among the less somber and more outgoing sculptures of Dynasty XVIII.

In the Middle Kingdom the placing of statues of deities in temples meant that the gods were more accessible to private persons. Even the tomb decoration of the New Kingdom testifies to a greater evolution in that direction. This may be seen, for example, in the reliefs and paintings of private people worshiping deities (Cat. 57b, upper left: the deceased standing before Osiris and the funerary deities known as the sons of Horus), and in the tomb statues of figures holding stelae inscribed with hymns to the sun. The trend is even clearer in temple sculptures such as that of Senenmut (Cat. 54) where a figure is actually shown holding a symbol of a deity. The presentation of a divine image, which is also a cryptogram of the name of Senenmut's sovereign, shows how closely the private could now be associated with the royal and the divine. Such iconography is unknown in the private statuary of earlier periods; the very pose, although still a stiff symbolic gesture, heralds the appearance of a new, dynamic element in the arts.

As the XVIIIth Dynasty progressed, Egypt became increasingly more wealthy and the Egyptians, at least those members of the upper classes for whom the major monuments were made, acquired a greater taste for the elegant and the sophisticated. This is only partly evident in the statuary of Tuthmosis III's successor, Amenhotep II, because in general the style established under Hatshepsut and Tuthmosis III continued during his reign. Some sculptures, such as Cat. 55, however, have narrower eyes, straighter brows and a more suave appearance in comparison with, for example, the face of Senenmut (Cat. 54). Others show somewhat less stylized and more naturalistically modeled bodies. These tendencies became more evident in the reign of the next king, Tuthmosis IV. By the time of his successor, Amenhotep III, most sculptures, royal and private, have quite a refined air. The figures generally wear elaborate wigs, jewelry, and garments; and their faces display elongated, elegant eyes, and highly ornamental brows.

The same refinement found in the statuary is also apparent in contemporary tomb paintings (Cat. 57), which display great richness in terms of design and coloring. The same is true of the minor arts (Cat. 58 and 59). The decoration of a vessel such as Cat. 58 reveals the degree to which the art of Dynasty XVIII, more than that of past ages, had developed a liking for forms based on curved lines and compositions rendering action. Needless to say, a degree of elegance and richness had always been displayed in the minor arts. However, earlier XVIIIth Dynasty creations in this field (Cat. 51 and 52) do not display the same exuberance as those of the later XVIIIth Dynasty (Cat. 72 and 74), which sometimes take on an almost rococo intricacy and playfulness (Cat. 75).

Other developments in the art were of equal importance. For example, scenes of the deceased at their official duties and in the presence of the king became more frequent. Also, the strict dependence upon outline in painting began to give way to another style. Now the figures are not just filled in with flat washes, but are built up with broader, sketchier masses of color—creating greater varieties of texture and, to a limited extent, of space and modeling. As time passed the artists also came to achieve a greater unity and depth in their compositions, by sometimes deviating from the age-old system of dividing walls into horizontal bands of decoration, by having figures interact with each other, by depicting specific poses and gestures, by placing figures in or around architectural settings, and by having more figures overlap. No longer are human beings drawn as hieroglyph-like symbols isolated within their own contours, but more as figures in a real world.

These then were some of the ways Egyptian art and culture had changed and was changing in the XVIIIth Dynasty when the most remarkable of Egyptian kings, Akhenaten, ascended the throne and instigated so many radical changes that his reign, from 1378 to 1362 B.C., in many ways constitutes a short separate era: the Amarna Period, called so after Tell el Amarna, the modern name of the site in Middle Egypt where Akhenaten erected a new capital city.

As might be expected in an essentially cloudless region where the sun so visibly and dramatically brings life to the land each day, the cult of the sun god Re was of great antiquity and had once risen to great prominence in the Old Kingdom. From the beginning of the New Kingdom the cult of Re once again became extremely important, even in the funerary practices of private persons. From the reign of Amenhotep II on, the Aten, the physical disk of the sun in which the power of Re became manifest, came to be the deity of a royal cult. It was the Aten, or rather Re in the form of the Aten, who became the god Akhenaten came to honor above and to the exclusion of all others.

When Akhenaten ascended the throne he did so as Amenhotep IV, a name in honor of Amun, the supreme god of Thebes. It was after several years on the throne that he founded his new capital where his god, the Aten, might be lord of his own domain; and about the same time the king changed his name to Akhenaten in honor of this god. Later in his reign Akhenaten launched an attack against some of the gods, especially Amun, by having the god's name erased from temples and other monuments.

This persecution of the older gods and elevation to supremacy of the new god, the Aten, gave Akhenaten the appearance of being a monotheist. However, Akhenaten and his wife, Queen Nefertiti, may have considered themselves as divine, and may have been so regarded by their followers. The larger residences at Tell el Amarna contained shrines housing images of the Aten with the royal family; and the inscriptions and representations make it clear that while the royal family prayed and offered to the Aten, their subjects prayed to them as intermediaries or as incarnations of the god, or as deities themselves.

Whatever the basic nature of the religion, the art of the Amarna Period was greatly different from the art of the past. For example, the royal family's exclusive access to the god appears to have obviated the need for private temple sculptures. Equally striking are the changes religion wrought in the iconography of temple and tomb decoration. The main theme of older temple decoration was retained: the reciprocal relationship between royalty and deity expressed in the king's presentation of offerings to the god (Cat. 34), who grants life and other benefits in return (Cat. 35). Now, however, the only god shown is the Aten, represented as a sun disk from which descend rays of light ending in human hands, often holding signs of life and power (Cat. 62 and 66).

With this basic element of iconography are associated scenes of the royal family in other rituals connected with the worship of the Aten, as well as scenes from nature relating to that worship. Indeed, all aspects of life are represented, including intimate scenes of the royal family (Cat. 69)—as if their entire existence and that of the city around them were one gigantic ritual glorifying the Aten. If in the past the real life of kings had become part of the timeless realm of the gods, in the temples at Tell el Amarna that real life came to dominate. The scenes of the daily round in Amarna Period temples remind one, in a way, of the appearance of such scenes in the solar temples of Dynasty V. It seems that various times in Egypt the cult of the sun gave rise to an artistic repertoire that reflected the sun's all-encompassing power.

Essentially the same themes appear in the private tombs at Tell el Amarna. Gone are the representations of the deceased offering to the gods and reflections of the belief in a godlike existence as Osiris in the next world. Instead, the deceased is promised a ghostlike continuation of life as it was led on earth. To be sure these scenes have links to the tomb decoration of the earlier XVIIIth Dynasty. Even then representations of the king had begun to appear in tombs and, as was the case at Tell el Amarna, the scenes chosen had to do with some aspect of the officials' service to the king (Fig. 11). But now the king had come to dominate all aspects of tomb decoration as if—as in the old Kingdom—he was the most important god.

Indeed, Akhenaten's father, Amenhotep III appears already to have embarked upon a deliberate policy of enhancing the status of the kingship. Ruler of an extremely prosperous and powerful country, early in his reign he abandoned the battlefield and turned his attention to the construction of grandiose monuments. Unlike most Egyptian kings, Amenhotep III also stressed his own divinity during his lifetime; to a lesser extent, this also seems to have been true of his wife Tiye.

Queens had always played an important role in Egypt—increasingly during the earlier New Kingdom and especially in the time of Tiye and Nefertiti. Both women appear to have been prominent in the religious and public affairs of the day; and one of the most striking features of the art of the Amarna Period is the manner in which Nefertiti and the royal princesses, with or without Akhenaten, are represented worshiping the Aten.

The appearance of a new iconography, almost from the beginning of Akhenaten's reign, was accompanied by a contemporary and equally dramatic change in the style of the art. Most striking is the untraditional manner in which the king was represented, highly individualized with full breasts, protruding stomach, large hips and thighs, long nose, full mouth, and drooping chin (Cat. 62, 64, 66, and Fig. 11). One must assume that these striking features reflect the king's true appearance; but whether he more closely resembled the earlier representations (Cat. 62) or later, less realistic images (Cat. 64-66) cannot be determined. This repertoire of physical appearance was primarily reserved for the king, for Nefertiti and, to a lesser extent, for their daughters. Perhaps such features were considered a sign of the god's special favor; in a relief made very early in the reign a solar deity is represented with the same peculiar physique. In the beginning of Akhenaten's reign representations of the head of Nefertiti are very like those of her husband. In later years, as the style of Amarna art became more idealizing, Nefertiti looked less and less like the king (Cat. 63 and 69). It is these later representations that show her as a woman considered beautiful.

If the specific features of Akhenaten were not reproduced in sculptures of all persons of whom statues were made, the more naturalistic approach implied did spread to many aspects of visual representation. Not all the elements of the traditional style were eliminated. For example, figures within the same scene were still drawn on different scales according to their importance; and the human torso and face were generally shown from multiple viewpoints (Fig. 11). But increasingly, figures were now represented in more natural scenery; were interrelated in actions, sometimes of an emotional nature (Cat. 69) rather than in formal attitudes (Cat. 19); and were integrated more fully into large settings (Cat. 67 and Fig. 11).

In fact, art lost a good deal of the character of writing—with separate statements strung together to tell a story—and took on more the quality of momentary reality. Fewer inscriptions accompany the scenes and are rendered more summarily than in earlier times. In such a stereotyped representation as the king offering, the deity is now shown simultaneously, rather than in a separate scene, bestowing his gift in return.

The contrast between the art of the Amarna Period and that of the preceding period may also be seen by comparing a relief made early in Akhenaten's reign (Cat. 62) with a sculpture in the elegant, idealizing style current under Amenhotep III (Cat. 61). The latter work is dated by inscription to the early years of Akhenaten's reign and indicates that there was at least some overlapping of styles. In fact, inasmuch as there may have been a coregency of Akhenaten and his father, the two styles may have coexisted for quite some time.

The history of the late Amarna Period is obscure; approximately seventeen years after he had become king, Akhenaten died, and the throne came to be occupied by a young male of the royal line named Tutankhaten. He and his successors were faced with major tasks. Whether Akhenaten's motive for attacking the other gods was religious fervor or a deliberate attempt to raise the status of kingship over that of the priest-hoods, its effect would have been to weaken the latter. It would also have caused severe problems in the country, for the temples were key institutions in Egypt's economy. By the time Tutankhaten died at about nineteen, he had changed his name to Tutankhamen in honor of Amun, had moved the court from Tell el Amarna to Memphis, had restored the cults of the older gods, and was taking steps to revitalize the country. The young king's policies were probably shaped by Ay, eventually his successor and apparently the father of Nefertiti. He in turn was followed as king by Horemheb, who had been general of the army under Tutankhamen.

The art of Dynasty XVIII after the Amarna Period encompasses a brief continuation of Amarna forms, a return to more orthodox features, and a blending of the Amarna and a more traditional style. After the reign of Tutankhamen, the traditional style predominated.

With the exception of Tell el Amarna itself and of Karnak during the early part of Akhenaten's reign, Memphis and its cemetery at Saqqara are among the few sites elsewhere in Egypt where Akhenaten's style flourished during his lifetime and retained a good many of its specific features for even a brief time after his death. For example, a relief from this region, probably made under Tutankhamen (Cat. 70), displays in its realistic rendering of old age, as well as in details such as the sharp collarbone (Cat. 63), a continuation of Amarna tradition.

In the reign of Tutankhamen, the style of Amarna was on the wane in the Nile Valley. After his death, even in Memphis, it lingered on mainly in facial features (Cat. 71) and a more naturalistic treatment of figures. However, there are two major exceptions to this generalization as we shall see below.

With the death of Horemheb, Dynasty XVIII ended and the throne passed into the hands of a family from the Delta, which founded Dynasty XIX. Dynasties XIX and XX are called the Ramesside Period because eleven of their kings were named Ramesses. After the brief reign of Ramesses I, the second and third kings of kings of Dynasty XIX, Sety I and Ramesses II, made great progress in restoring a prosperous administration as well as some of Egypt's standing outside the borders in Asia. Under the next king, Merenptah, Egypt was forced to defend itself against a first wave of invaders from Libya, Asia Minor, and the Aegean. Dynasty XIX ended in brief reigns and dynastic intrigue; but the land prospered again with Ramesses III, the second king of Dynasty XX. He successfully defended Egypt from a Libyan invasion as well as one by a great coalition of Western Asian and Aegean peoples who destroyed many of the states in the Near East.

Ramesses III's victory over the Libyans, however, was defensive in nature and only temporarily ended the pressure on Egypt from outside her borders. Later in Dynasty XX marauding bands of Libyans roamed Upper Egypt and large numbers of their compatriots settled in the Western Delta. The authority of the kings was declining, accompanied by a rise in power of the priesthood of Amun. Lavish gifts from the pharaohs of the New Kingdom had made that priesthood extremely wealthy, and in late Dynasty XX Amun's High Priests assumed powers rivaling those of the king. In fact, for some years during the reign of the last Ramesside king, the High Priest of Amun, Herihor, adopted royal titles. Herihor did not displace his sovereign by this action, and it was only in certain temple reliefs at Thebes that he played the role of king. However, the fact that he was not only High Priest of Amun but General of the Army indicates into whose hands the control of the country was passing. When Dynasty XX ended it was the High Priests of Amun who, although nominally subject to a dynasty of kings residing at Tanis in the Delta, ruled Upper Egypt.

Thus began the Third Intermediate Period: Dynasties XXI (1080–945 B.C.), XXII (945–715 B.C.), XXIII (818–720 B.C.), XXIV (727–715 B.C), and the early part of Dynasty XXV. During Dynasty XXI the High Priests of Amun, related by marriage to the kings at Tanis, ruled the southern part of the country. The rulers of Dynasties XXII–XXIV were thoroughly Egyptianized Libyan kings, the descendants of people who had settled in Egypt in Ramesside times. In the early stages of this period the country was relatively unified and strong, but it later disintegrated into two rival dynasties (XXII and XXIII) in both parts of the country, and smaller local rulers, mostly Libyan chieftains in the Western Delta. Under such conditions it was possible for kings from Nubia first to extend their power over Upper Egypt and then eventually to take over the entire country, in Dynasty XXV.

Early Ramesside art in Dynasty XIX is marked by major building projects undertaken by Sety I. But they do not compare in size and number with those carried out for Ramesses II during his nearly seven decades of kingship. In their colossal scale many of the latter's works reflect the great stress he placed on his own divinity during his lifetime.

The monuments of both Sety I and Ramesses II show an interesting dichotomy in style. To a great extent their artists turned for inspiration to the monuments of the pre-Amarna kings of Dynasty XVIII, especially to those of King Amenhotep III. Like the artists of that great king, those of Sety I and Ramesses II often created works of great elegance (Cat. 78 and Fig. 1); but such reliefs as Cat. 77 and some of the contemporary statuary are, in comparison with Dynasty XVIII work, characterized by a drier, more precise style. Even works such as Fig. 1 have a coldness only partially relieved by their sometimes elegantly sweeping lines. On the other hand, although this is not true of the majority of the new works, the influences of the style of the Amarna Period were not totally supressed. For example, the bold sunk relief modeling of a slab such as Cat. 77 is, although flatter, ultimately dependent upon the reliefs of the Amarna Period (Cat. 62) and its aftermath (Cat. 76). These reliefs, unlike their predecessors which were restricted to one or two planes and gave an essentially flat appearance, depended on deeply cut, overlapping forms which derive some of their effect from a modeling produced by a play of light and shade. In contrast to what is seen in the other works of Sety I and Ramesses II, the legacy of Amarna was very strong in the great battle scenes (Fig. 4). In these, hundreds of figures are united in one large landscape setting; in the reliefs of Sety I many figures convey elements of drama and emotion characteristic of the art of Akhenaten.

These royal pieces set a pattern seldom deviated from in later Dynasty XIX and XX, except for some reliefs of Ramesses III where the workmanship was often of relatively low technical quality.

With the decline in royal power, the rise in the power of the priesthoods and the worsening conditions in the land, some remarkable changes took place in the realm of private sculptures. Those preserved, mainly block statues, are primarily from temples. Like other statue types, they were increasingly represented as holding images or symbols of gods. In private tombs, with few exceptions by late Dynasty XIX, the scenes of daily life of the deceased had all but vanished. The walls were now almost entirely covered with scenes relating to the burial of and offering to the dead, and of the deceased's communion with the gods (Cat. 80). As in the case with most royal relief and painting of the Ramesside Period, the majority of the private works give a basic impression of flatness. In painting the figures generally were outlines filled in with plain washes of color; in relief the carving tends to be executed on a single plane. However, as in the great Ramesside battle scenes some private works, such as Cat. 80, reflect the influence of Amarna art in the creation of a sense of depth by overlapping forms and the cutting of different areas of the relief at different depths.

Not all the creations of the Ramesside Period—especially not the minor arts—show a dry formality. An object such as Cat. 82, if simpler than its late XVIIIth Dynasty prototype (Cat. 75), is still ornate and quite lively. And in numerous works of the time we find not only vibrant sketches but also a tendency toward satire (Cat. 84) inspired by the unsettled social conditions of the time.

The Third Intermediate Period, despite the unsettled political conditions of the time, was not marked by an overall decline in the quality of the arts. To be sure, in the later part of the period, when the political fragmentation of the land increased, some work produced at sites other than the major artistic centers was quite crude. On the other hand, a stela such as Cat. 88 is still quite competently worked, although it displays some inelegancies of carving, as evidenced in the poor modeling of the figures. The royal and priestly building activities of the era were modest compared with those of former periods, but the relief decoration, even from the latter part of the period, generally followed Ramesside style. Sometimes the quality equaled or even surpassed that which is found in Dynasty XX.

It is harder to judge the state of royal statuary during the Third Intermediate Period, for very little of it has been preserved. A head of King Osorkon II (889–866 B.C.) of Dynasty XXII is comparable to most royal sculpture of Dynasty XX, while an earlier head such as Cat. 85 shows no appreciable decline in quality compared with its Dynasty XX precursors. It does, however, differ in that the face is narrower and more delicate and the skull longer, as is found in contemporary reliefs of kings and High Priests of Amun. There are also a few fine bronzes, perhaps the finest ever made in Egypt. Some are quite large, but even the smaller ones (Cat. 87) are of better quality than the mass-produced bronzes of later times.

There is almost no private tomb relief or painting known, for few tombs seem to have been decorated in the Third Intermediate Period. But what little tomb decoration is preserved, as well as lavishly painted papyri and coffins of the period, show that this was not a lost art. It too continued and developed its own variants on Ramesside forms and style.

We have almost no evidence for private statuary in Dynasty XXI; but from the latter part of the Third Intermediate Period, both in the North and in the South, statues were made which generally followed Ramesside forms and, even if displaying some lack of originality, were technically on a par with most private sculpture of Dynasty XX. A few of these were distinctly archaizing and even older statues were usurped for use, drawing on material as far back as the Middle Kingdom. There may also be observed in the minor arts of the Third Intermediate Period archaizing tendencies which became more prevalent in the art of the Late Period, which followed. Indeed, archaizing features also occur in a new style employed by the Nubian kings of Dynasty XXV.

47

Cat. 47. Dagger. Its discovery in a New Kingdom palace and similarity to a dagger buried with Queen Ahhotep (time of King Ahmose) indicate an early Dynasty XVIII date for this elegant refinement of a dagger type which appeared in the Middle Kingdom. Bronze, with ivory pommel. Length 23.3 cm.

Cat. 48. King Amenhotep I with the Crown of Upper Egypt. Although the cartouche before his face is not preserved, we can identify this second king of Dynasty XVIII on the basis of stylistically identical raised reliefs (in the same creamy white Theban limestone) bearing his name. That style is based on an early Dynasty XII Theban monument which, as evident in the eyes, nose, and ears (Cat. 32 and 33a) continued Dynasty XI traditions.

Many royal works of early Dynasty XVIII archaize, or go back to older forms. Theban artists, trying to regain their skills after a troubled period of artistic decline, often turned to the Middle Kingdom monuments of Mentuhotep II and Sesostris I (both long since deified) because of their beauty and accessibility. The XVIIIth Dynasty art also served both magical and propaganda purposes by associating the newly united country's Theban leaders with great Theban kings of yore. Limestone. Height 31.0 cm.

Cat. 49. Statue of a man named Ahmose Ruru. One of the two names of Tuthmosis III (rear and right side) was recut in antiquity, and both of the names of Tuthmosis I were also reinscribed. Since Tuthmosis III would later in his reign have replaced Hatshepsut's name with his own or Tuthmosis I's, this sculpture can be dated earlier in Dynasty XVIII, during the time of his joint reign with Hatshepsut. Stylistic details such as the broad face and its features fit well with this date, as does the type of figure, with one hand over the heart and the other clutching the long tight coat, known from other sculptures of the time and based on a Middle Kingdom prototype. Gray metamorphic slate. Height 38.1 cm.

49

48

Cat. 50a-b. Block statue of Min, Overseer of Weavers. Stylistic elements such as the wide striated wig, broad face, and facial features permit dating in the first half of Dynasty XVIII. Although not identical to, and somewhat more elegant than, the corresponding features of Cat. 49, the similarities associate the two statues closely in time. As in other Dynasty XVIII block statues, the feet are covered by the robe, a tradition continued from the later block statues of the Middle Kingdom. Gray green slate. Height 23.3 cm.

50b

50a

Cat. 51. One of a pair of clappers for marking musical time. The design reflects the Egyptian tendency to give objects—or decorate them with—forms expressing and religiously or magically associated with their function. Hands clap. A head of Hathor, goddess of music and dance, is appropriate to a sistrum (Cat. 80). A Hathor head or here, one step further, Hathor as sistrum, is appropriate to a clapper. Probably early Dynasty XVIII. Ivory. Length 18.2 cm.

Cat. 52. Bowl. The exterior represents a lotus; the interior is decorated with a design of a lotus pool. If the pool represents the primordial waters and the lotus the first life to arise therefrom, both pool and plants would be magical symbols of the creative powers of life. Early Dynasty XVIII. Blue and black glazed faience. Diameter 26.3 cm.

51

52

Cat. 53. Scribe's palette with slot for brushes and depression for pigments. From a cemetery, and inscribed with prayers for the scribe Nebiry, it was part of the burial equipment of a member of Egypt's most respected profession. The deities invoked are Thoth and Seshat, Lord and Mistress of Writing, and Onuris and Mehit, local deities. The cartouche of Tuthmosis III of Dynasty XVIII indicates a date in his reign. Wood. Length 38.0 cm.

54a

53

54b

54a-b. Statue of Senenmut. Hatshepsut's most famous and powerful official kneels holding a cobra crowned with cow horns and sun disk, resting upon raised arms. The texts identify the serpent as the goddess Renenutet; they describe Senenmut's proffering her image as an act benefiting his Queen; and they invoke benefices for Senenmut from the goddess after death. Hatshepsut's name appears on his shoulder; the cobra with its accompanying symbols is also a cryptogram of her name.

Contemporary with Cat. 49, Senenmut's statue displays no similar dependence upon Middle Kingdom art. The proffering pose is new; the shape of the face, curved brows, and to an extent the aquiline nose are features seen in somewhat earlier New Kingdom reliefs as well as sculptures of Hatshepsut. But the strongly hooked nose, known from other works of Senenmut, seems to be based on his actual appearance. New also is the fact that this official owned over twenty statues of himself, the first private person since the Old Kingdom known to own so many. Dynasty XVIII. Gray granite. Height 47.2 cm.

Cat. 55. King Amenhotep II. The calm, idealized facial types created for his immediate predecessors strongly influenced the images created for Amenhotep II as well as contemporary private sculpture. However, his sculptures often have, as in this face from an over life-size statue, a straighter nose and eyebrows and a more serious expression. Dynasty XVIII. Red granite. Height 31.1 cm.

55

Cat. 56. Bust of a lioness-headed goddess. With over five hundred similar sculptures known, this bust, crowned with sun disk and uraeus, may safely be attributed to a seated figure of Sakhmet, "The Powerful," the destroyer of the enemies of the sun and the king. A few of these statues may be dated to Dynasty XXII on the basis of their texts and iconography. But the vast majority, including our bust, were made for King Amenhotep III. Many figures are still standing in the temple of the goddess Mut at Karnak, where Sakhmet was, according to an inscription, "united with" that main consort of Amun (Cat. 87); but it has been suggested that they originally stood in the King's funerary temple whence some were brought in Dynasty XXI, and that there were 730 such figures—two for each day in the year—constituting a sculptural version of the double litany of names pronounced each day for this goddess. Dynasty XVIII. Gray diorite. Height 74.3 cm.

56

57b

Cat. 57a. The Lady Thepu. Painting, as distinct from painted relief, was used for tomb decoration as early as Predynastic times but was most popular for this purpose in the New Kingdom. Under Tuthmosis IV and Amenhotep III in Dynasty XVIII Egyptian painters achieved their greatest skill and the medium its greatest freedom. From the reign of King Amenhotep III, this painting of the Lady Thepu, with her elegant wig, lavish jewelry, diaphanous garment, wisp of hair over eye and brow, and arm showing through both wig and shawl, fits well in the opulent context of an Egypt made wealthy and more sophisticated by its military, commercial, and cultural contacts with neighboring countries.

Though the mother of an adult son, she is portrayed, as befits the noble dead, in the ideal blush of eternal youth. This figure comes from a Theban tomb where Thepu was shown assisting her son Nebamun (one of two sculptors for whom this tomb was decorated) in making a burnt offering to a number of deities from whom blessings are invoked (Cat. 57b, not in exhibition). Their action is an episode in the Beautiful Feast of the Valley, an annual ritual centering around the visit of the god Amun (Cat. 87) to shrines in the cemeteries at Thebes. Coinciding with that presence of magical benefit to the deceased, various rituals were conducted in the tombs, including a banquet (partially visible to the right of Thepu in Cat. 57b) in which the dead were believed to participate. Dynasty XVIII. Paint on gesso over mud plaster. Height 30.2 cm.

57a

Cat. 58. Jar. The decoration, pale blue against the buff ground, consists of bands and petal friezes framing a marshscape of water fowl, leaping bull calves, and nude young women in papyrus boats. The decoration of this vessel is in keeping with the motifs and spirit of much art of the New Kingdom, one of the two periods—the other was the Predynastic Period—with elaborately painted pottery. Made about the time of King Amenhotep III, this jar in part reflects the poorly preserved palace painting of his time. Dynasty XVIII. Painted pottery. Height 29.6 cm.

Cat. 59. Figure of a frog. This amphibian may have been made solely for its visual appeal. However, as frogs were symbols of life and rebirth, and as somewhat similar figures of frogs bear propitious inscriptions, it may have been an amulet. The combination of dark and turquoise blue glaze is characteristic of the time of King Amenhotep III. Dynasty XVIII. Dark blue faience with brown eyes and light blue body stripes. Height 5.3 cm.

58

59

Cat. 60. Statuette of the Songstress Mi. This figure, from a tomb containing objects bearing the name of both Amenhotep III and IV, wears a heavy wig and a diaphanous pleated dress, and once had a gold collar. Dynasty XVIII. Wood, with gilt button earrings and traces of a gold leaf bracelet. Height 15.6 cm.

So much of Egyptian art was made for the king or directly influenced by royal art that it is generally possible, without denying the existence of other works, to speak of "the" style of the times. Cat. 61 and 62 were certainly made during Amenhotep IV's early years on the throne, before he changed his name to Akhenaten; but 61 is in an elegant, idealizing style of the time of King Amenhotep III, and 62 in the far different style of the early art created for Akhenaten. Cat. 60, possibly contemporary with 61 and 62, is in a style of the Amarna Period, as evidenced by its physiognomy and quite naturalistic treatment of the body with slightly sagging breasts and large buttocks. Nevertheless, it stands somewhat apart from works known to have been made for Akhenaten. This overlapping of styles reflects either a transition in the art following the change from the reign of Amenhotep III to that of Amenhotep IV, or the coexistence of different styles made for kings who may have been coregents.

60

61

Cat. 61. Bust from a seated statue. Dated by the name of King Amenhotep IV on his right arm. Clearly an important personage from the size and quality of his sculpture, this unidentified official is represented wearing a double wig, pleated robe, necklace, and gold armlets of a type awarded by kings for valor. Dynasty XVIII. Gray granite. Height 56.0 cm.

Cat. 62. Sunk relief of King Amenhotep IV. The King raises his arm in worship of the solar disk, the Aten, whose rays grant him life (ankh) and support his uraeus. Dynasty XVIII. Sandstone with traces of gesso and paint. Height 17.0 cm.

Cat. 63. Sculptor's model. The king (left) and queen may be identified as Akhenaten and Nefertiti on the basis of their resemblance to inscribed representations of that royal couple. Pierced by a hole for suspension, this object was created by a master craftsman to serve as a model for other artists. It is in the later style of the Amarna Period, characterized by a softening of the stylizations of Akhenaten's earlier years (Cat. 62). Dynasty XVIII. Limestone. Height 15.7 cm.

62

63

Cat. 64. Statuette of a king. The long nose; sensuous, drooping lips; heavy jaw, breasts, stomach, and buttocks; and the spindly calves identify this figure as Akhenaten. Executed in the later style of the Amarna Period, it was found in a private house at Tell el Amarna, where it may have been enshrined as an image of the King as god or intermediary to the god. Dynasty XVIII. Painted limestone with gilded diadem, uraeus, collar, and apron. Height 21.9 cm.

Cat. 65. Head of a *shawabti* of Akhenaten. The face, unlike those of some of the cruder magical servant figures of this type made for Akhenaten, resembles major sculptures of the King in its slanted eyes and full mouth with pendulous lower lip. Dynasty XVIII. Yellow limestone. Height 6.4 cm.

65

Cat. 66a-b. Sunk relief. Akhenaten offering a bouquet to the Aten. In return for the offering, one of the Aten's rays grants life to the King in the form of an *ankh*-sign. Behind Akhenaten, in the musician's role common for priestesses, his daughter rattles a sistrum (Cat. 66b). Carved in the softer style of the later Amarna Period, she has, as is common for representations of Akhenaten's daughters, an elongated skull and less unusual facial features than her father. Akhenaten's face, the cartouches on his body, and the inscription above the princess have been deliberately erased. Dynasty XVIII. Limestone with mostly modern pigment. Height 23.1 cm.

64

66a

66b

67

68

Cat. 67. Sunk relief of King Akhenaten's palace kitchens. Represented within a large architectural setting, a compositional device commonly employed in the Amarna Period, are bakers, brewers, and men carrying a wine vessel toward a courtyard swept by a servant. Dynasty XVIII. Limestone with modern red paint. Height 22.0 cm.

Cat. 68. Sunk relief of three antelopes. From one of Akhenaten's temples, it may have been part of a hunting scene or a view of Akhenaten's city and its immediate environs. The detailed naturalistic modeling is typically Amarnan; but because Egyptian art generally depicts animals from a single viewpoint, they are usually more naturalistic than human figures. Dynasty XVIII. Limestone with mostly modern paint. Height 23.1 cm.

Cat. 69. Sunk relief of mother and child. In this block from a large scene, Queen Nefertiti is shown, kissing a daughter under the life-giving rays of the Aten. This is one of the few representations of a kiss known in Egyptian art. Only during the Amarna Period were emotional relationships between royalty portrayed in a realistic fashion or given such prominence. Nefertiti's face has been deliberately damaged and most of the inscription, but not the "Aten" in her daughter's name, erased. Dynasty XVIII. Painted limestone. Height 23.2 cm.

69

70

Cat. 70. Sunk relief of an elderly man. Before or under a kiosk, an important personage makes a gesture of greeting or introduction. The unusual realistic rendering of old age is dependent, both in concept and details, upon the art of the Amarna Period but is not wholly in the style created for King Akhenaten. It was carved during or shortly after the Amarna Period at Memphis, one of the relatively few sites where the Amarna style is known to have flourished. Dynasty XVIII. Limestone. Height 14.4 cm.

Cat. 71a-b. Block statue of Yii. In general the Amarna style was rapidly modified under Akhenaten's successors in Dynasty XVIII. The forms of the eyes and mouth of this sculpture (one of the very few made under King Ay) reflect sculptures of Tutankhamen, themselves dependent upon works of Akhenaten (Cat. 65). The sculptural type, however, represents a return to traditional forms. Dynasty XVIII. Limestone. Height 47.2 cm.

71a

71b

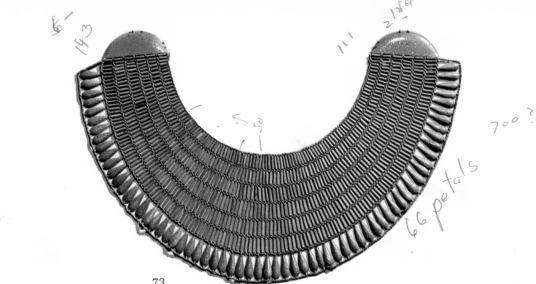

73

72

Cat. 72. Mirror with handle in the form of a Nubian girl. The disk was originally gilded. Dynasty XVIII is famous for luxury objects, and the young female nude was one of its favorite motifs. Mirrors were valuable, as is vividly indicated by a text which lists as a calamity of a period of social upheaval the fact that women once poor had become able to afford them. Late Dynasty XVIII. Bronze. Height 22.2 cm.

Cat. 73. Broad collar necklace. Necklaces were commonly worn or represented as being worn by gods, kings, and private persons from the Old Kingdom onward. This is a perfectly preserved example. In addition to their function as adornment, such collars were believed to protect their wearers. Several examples were found in the tomb of King Tutankhamen, to whose reign this necklace may be dated. Deep blue faience. Width 36.6 cm.

Cat. 74. Monkey with ball or fruit. This figure is one of the small luxury items for which Dynasty XVIII is famous. It is said to come from Tell el Amarna where other figures of playful simians, although executed in a different style, were found. Variants of this motif are known from tomb reliefs and paintings of the Old Kingdom on into the New Kingdom. Blue faience. Height 5.4 cm.

74

Cat. 75. Spoon. The scoop is in the form of a lotus blossom and mandrake fruit. The handle is shaped like a formal bouquet. Such objects, found in burials, were used for making actual or symbolic offerings to the gods. Both lotus and bouquet were symbols of life and suitable gifts to gods (Cat. 66) and mortals (Cat. 57b, lower right), and their use as decorative motifs was therefore appropriate to an implement used in the making of offerings. This spoon is in the almost rococo style best associated with late Dynasty XVIII. Wood with ivory and blue paste inlays. Length 29.5 cm.

Cat. 76. Wounded Nubian soldier supported by a comrade. The face of a third figure is preserved in the upper left. Partial parallels for this group exist in battle scenes of Ramesses II. If these figures came from such subsidiary scenes of routs or processions of prisoners, the total composition would have been extremely large. But the battle scenes of the New Kingdom (Fig. 4), if continuing and expanding upon the Amarna tradition of large landscape settings, provide no parallels for many of the features of this relief. For example, both the degree of emotion and psychological contact between figures expressed especially by the parted lips, and the bold, overlapping forms which are partially modeled by the shadows they cast, argue for a date in the time of Akhenaten or, more likely, Horemheb. Late Dynasty XVIII. Sandstone. Height 39.4 cm.

75

Cat. 77. King Ramesses II. The position of the King's arms indicates that he was shown making an offering (Cat. 106 and 107). This piece comes from the temple of King Ramesses II at Abydos; it closely resembles other sunk reliefs there. With the exception of the creases on the neck (Cat. 63), there are few stylistic details here which remind one strongly of the art of Amarna. The flattish forms and bland, idealized facial features resemble instead some reliefs of Ramesses' father, King Sety I—themselves marked by a return to pre-Amarna forms. Dynasty XIX. Painted limestone. Height 42.5 cm.

76

77

78

79

Cat. 78. Standard in the form of a sphinx with two uraei. Combining two potent protective symbols, this object was a part of some cult apparatus, probably a sacred boat of a god, such as is often shown in temple reliefs (Fig. 7). The profile view, in its great elegance of form, reflects one of the main strengths of Ramesside art. Dynasty XIX. Bronze with traces of gilding. Height of sphinx 12.8 cm.

Cat. 79. Canopic jar of Thenry, Supervisor of Works for Ramesses II. Thenry's command of royal artisans explains the unusually high quality of such a common object. Based on contemporary works but altered—eyes smaller and higher up on the face, nose larger—its features have an individuality lacking in most sculptures of the time. In the panel, Thenry worships Imsety, the funerary deity represented by this vessel made for the burial of Thenry's liver. Dynasty XIX. Alabaster. Height 45.9 cm.

Cat. 80. Sunk relief of nobleman worshiping. This figure comes from a tomb at Saqqara, decorated about the time of King Ramesses II. It must have formed part of a scene common in Ramesside tombs: the deceased, accompanied by a female relative with sistrum, offering to the gods. Its extreme serenity and formal elegance are found in many other fine works of the period. The creation of slight spatial relationships by the cutting of the rear profile deeper than the front profile (where the face emerges before the wig) is not a general feature of the art of the time. Dynasty XIX. Painted limestone. Height 52.0 cm.

80

81

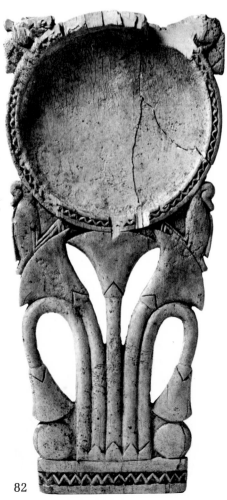

82

Cat. 81. Sunk relief. A woman, followed by female musicians, is represented receiving a libation from an elevated figure (perhaps a goddess in a tree). It is often possible to determine the type of scene from which a fragment comes because most subjects were not unique to one temple or tomb. An identification has not yet proved possible for this sunk relief. It has, however, been suggested that the inscription above is a hymn being sung, mentioning a "uraeus of gold." Peculiarities of the inscriptions indicate a date later than the Ramesside Period, the era with which the style of the figures is best associated. Limestone. Height 30.8 cm.

Cat. 82. Ladle for offerings. This is an example of the sort of magical object represented also by Cat. 75. Its overall form may be related to that of ornate mirrors and may have been based, as with the mirrors, upon the sign of life (*ankh*). The motif of a solar disk rising atop plants from the water below is a symbol of the ever renewing power of life. Late New Kingdom. Ivory. Length 18.5 cm.

Cat. 83. Ostracon with bear and dwarf. Pottery fragments and limestone flakes were often used in place of costly papyrus for correspondence, artists' sketches, or students' practice work. The two motifs are somewhat dissimilar in style and differently oriented. The uncommon representation of a bear and unusual details of the dwarf may indicate they were sketches of interesting elements observed in some monument's decoration. Ramesside or earlier. Limestone. Dimensions: 20.0 by 21.0 cm.

Cat. 84. Ostracon with cat and mouse. Datable to late Dynasty XX on the basis of similar representations of that time, including papyri for which this might be a sketch or copy. Although the motif of cat as servant to a noble lady mouse might illustrate a lost fable it is also, in its reversal of natural roles, a satirical comment on the social disintegration of late Ramesside times. Limestone. Height 8.9 cm.

83

84

85

86

Cat. 85. Head of a man. The style of this head, its facial features, and long skull, argue for a date either in the late Ramesside Period or Dynasty XXI, two periods whose art is often similar but about which too little is known to permit a definite identification of the person here represented. The caplike crown with a slot for a lost metal uraeus proves he was a king or one of the high priests of Dynasty XXI at Thebes who in fact, and sometimes in title, ruled Upper Egypt. Red quartzite. Height 11.3 cm.

Cat. 86. Head of Taweret. From a figure of this goddess of childbirth in the form of a pregnant hippopotamus. Difficult to date for lack of close parallels, it is either from Dynasties XXI-XXV or, because of its rare material and precisely detailed modeling, from Dynasty XVIII. Black hematite. Height 2.4 cm.

Cat. 87. Statuette of Amun-Re of Thebes. Seldom inscribed and less prone to stylistic or iconographic change than statues of kings or nobles, bronze figures of deities are often difficult to date; but this image of Egypt's principal god from the New Kingdom onward may be attributed to Dynasty XXII because of its gold inlays, slim waist, low belt, and overall high quality. Bronze. Height 20.2 cm.

Cat. 88. Donation stela. In year 22 of the reign of King Sheshonq III, a ruler of Mendes erected this stela. It records a gift of land to a flautist of that city's divine owners. The ruler is shown offering a hieroglyph for "fields." Behind him stands the musician, identified by inscription and flute. The long text explains the event symbolized and invokes the deities represented before the flautist and his ruler to preserve the flautist's possession of the land. Anyone seizing the land, it is promised, shall be beheaded by the gods and his son deprived of his hereditary rights—but only after the villain and his wife are violated by an ass and the wife violates their children. Despite modern popular beliefs, such curses were rare in ancient Egypt. By his titles and by the feather atop his head the donor is identified as one of the Libyan chieftains who effectively controlled much of Egypt during the Third Intermediate Period. Dynasty XXII. Limestone. Height 52.3 cm.

87

88

page 97

89

Cat. 89. Plaque inscribed for King Iuput I or II. In its proportions, facial features, and costume, the figure closely resembles the representations of the Dynasty XXV Nubian conquerors of Egypt. Therefore, the style of this piece would argue for its attribution to King Iuput II of Late Dynasty XXIII because he, unlike the Iuput I of early Dynasty XXIII, was contemporary with early Dynasty XXV. The mixed nature of the art of this transitional period is indicated by a plaque from the same shrine, now in Edinburgh, which does not so clearly betray a Nubian influence. Green glazed faience. Height 29.3 cm.

V. The Late Period

The conquest of Egypt by kings from Nubia ushered in the last great era of Egyptian history and civilization: the Late Period (750–30 B.C.). Unlike most of the previous chronological divisions of Egyptian history, this was not an era of strong political unity and power. Indeed, the earlier part of the Late Period was marked by alternations between native rule and foreign domination.

The dynasty of Nubian kings (Dynasty XXV: 750–656 B.C.) was followed by the XXVIth Dynasty (664–525 B.C.), which developed from the rulership of a princely family of Sais in the Western Delta. Their last king, Psamtik III, was defeated in battle by the Achaemenid Persians who conquered Egypt and whose rule constitutes Dynasty XXVII (525–404 B.C.). Thereafter followed three Egyptian Dynasties (XXVIII: 404–399 B.C.; XXIX: 399–380 B.C.; XXX: 380–342 B.C.) of which only the last was strong enough to be conducive to the growth of art. When Dynasty XXX ended, Egypt once again came briefly under the domination of the Persians (Dynasty XXXI: 342–332 B.C.). Soon, however, the country was lost by them to Alexander the Great. This event marked the beginning of the second phase of the Late Period, years during which Egypt was governed by rulers of foreign origin. From Alexander's native Macedonia is derived the name for the time when Egypt formed part of his empire—the Macedonian Period (332–305 B.C.).

After Alexander's death in 323 B.C., Egypt was administered by a trusted Macedonian governor, Ptolemy Lagou; and when the empire broke apart it was ruled by Ptolemy I and his descendants who assumed the role of the ancient pharaohs of Egypt. Twelve kings of this line were named Ptolemy, hence the designation Ptolemaic Period (305–30 B.C.). The end came with the death of Cleopatra VII, the famous queen, and Egypt's conquest by the Romans. Thus, Egypt lost all its independence and thereafter became the property of the Imperial Roman family.

The length of the Late Period—about 700 years—and its unsettled political history manifests itself in the variety of art of the era. Yet, just as the alternation of foreign with domestic rule characterizes the political history of the period, so the art reflects a multitude of features both foreign and native. The three most noticeable stylistic features in Late Period art are the idealizing, the archaizing, and the realistic, all known in the art of earlier ages.

The Nubian conquerors of Dynasty XXV portrayed themselves in their inscriptions as true Egyptians. They established their superiority in Upper Egypt by adopting the spiritual kingdom of the god Amun at Thebes and by appointing a Nubian princess to be the god's divine consort.

That rulers from a kingdom on the Upper Nile, far from Egypt, could see themselves as true Egyptians and become accepted as such in Egypt is the result of a number of factors. Throughout the New Kingdom Nubia and the northern Sudan were controlled and administered by Egypt, and the inhabitants were partly Egyptianized. Important is the fact that by the time the Nubians entered Egypt as kings their principal deity had come to be a Nubian version of the Egyptian god Amun.

As has been noted before, with the exception of Akhenaten, the pharaohs of Egypt in the New Kingdom based their claim to the throne on the belief that they were the offspring of the god Amun. Their policies and achievements were credited to the god's direction and support. Under such conditions the priesthood of Amun had an important role to play, but was still subordinate to the king. As long as the rulers were strong they retained control of the interpretation of the god's will, took pride in their own human achievements, and assumed a more godlike role which probably reached its epitome in the reign of Akhenaten. After a decline under his XVIIIth Dynasty successors, this role was to some extent restored to the king by Sety I and Ramesses II. With the waning of royal power, especially after the reign of Ramesses III, the kings came to depend upon the support of the priesthood of Amun, forfeited their role as interpreters of the god's will; and in Dynasty XXI Upper Egypt was governed by the High Priests. In early Dynasty XXII the Libyan kings were able to contain the High Priests' power by limiting the territory they controlled. They installed relatives in this exalted office and—as had the kings of Dynasties XVIII and XIX—prevented the office from becoming an hereditary one. However, its control was still vital to the maintenance of royal authority in Upper Egypt. Such were the importance of this office and the independent position of Thebes that conflicts affecting the High Priesthood of Amun helped plunge the country into civil wars and political fragmentation.

This was the state of Upper Egypt when the Nubians arrived. Possibly they felt that they, under the aegis of their Amun, were intervening legitimately on their own behalf and on behalf of the Theban Amun. Unfortunately, we do not have any concrete evidence for the relations between Nubia and Thebes during the Third Intermediate Period, prior to the Nubian invasion of Egypt. Some links may have been maintained. At the very end of the Ramesside Period the High Priest Herihor (1100–1094 B.C.) also held the titles of Commander of the Army and Egyptian Viceroy of Nubia. At any rate, once the Nubian kings invaded Egypt, they adopted the traditional title of King of Upper and Lower Egypt; and they claimed that the right to control both countries had been granted to them by Amun of Napata, their capital on the Upper Nile, and by Amun of Thebes.

As the Nubians had long been exposed to Egyptian art of the New Kingdom, a time during which Egyptian temples were erected at many sites in the Sudan, much Nubian art was based on Egyptian styles and forms of the New Kingdom. The kings of Nubia, well after Ramesside times, still occasionally appeared in elaborate Ramesside garb. The most characteristic Nubian head covering—a skullcap with tabs in front of the ears, with (Cat. 90) or without (Cat. 89) headband—may have originated ultimately in the close-fitting caps worn by rulers of the Ramesside and Third Intermediate Periods (Cat. 85). Other elements of Nubian regalia, such as the use of double uraeus on a king's headgear (Cat. 90) rather than a single cobra (Cat. 64), have fewer prototypes in Egypt, but are nevertheless of Egyptian origin. The exact significance of the double uraeus is still uncertain, but it probably symbolizes rulership over Upper and Lower Egypt.

Not all Egyptianizing art created under the kings of Dynasty XXV, was based on New Kingdom precedents, however; some was archaizing. For example, King Taharqa, next to last king of Dynasty XXV, is known to have used workmen from Memphis in the construction of a temple in Nubia; and whole scenes which adorn its walls were copied from royal funerary monuments of the Old Kingdom. The most interesting subject of these Old Kingdom wall decorations is the defeat of Libyan enemies whose countrymen later had come to be the very rulers defeated by the Nubians.

It must be remembered that, despite the degree to which the Nubian kings of Dynasty XXV had been Egyptianized and continued or resurrected Egyptian artistic forms, they were not Egyptians. The precise origin of Nubian rulership is uncertain, but we can gain some idea of their early culture from a cemetery at El Kurru, below the Fourth Cataract of the Nile, where their burials, extending back to the late 10th Century B.C., have been uncovered. Here the earlier tombs are of a tumulus type, which has a long history in the southern Sudan. It is only in the tombs of those rulers who exercised power in Egypt that we see the rapid adaptation of some Egyptian burial customs, as for example the use of canopic jars (Cat. 79), *shawabtis* (Cat. 92), and numerous amulets in Egyptian style. Also, they employed pyramid-shaped superstructures for tombs, a form abandoned by Egyptian kings in the New Kingdom.

It must be noted, however, that many of the amulets and other decorative objects found in these Nubian tombs were non-Egyptian or Egyptianizing. For example, the ram's head may have been an Egyptian symbol of Amun; but the royal Nubian ram's head amulet (Cat. 91) was not of a type known earlier in Egypt.

To judge from what little has been preserved of the royal art of Dynasty XXV, a head such as Cat. 90 must have come from a striding statue much like those made for Egyptian rulers since the Old Kingdom (Fig. 10); perhaps it was even inspired by a sculpture of that period. The manner in which the face has been rather simply modeled, its straightforward gaze and somewhat idealizing physiognomy also lie within an Egyptian tradition reaching back to the Old Kingdom. Yet, even if the top of the head with its Nubian skullcap and double uraeus had not been preserved, it would be possible on the basis of its broad face and thick neck to identify this sculpture as the representation of a Nubian pharaoh. This adaptation of a specifically foreign physiognomy to Egyptian royal art constitutes the novel approach of the period.

Nubians had certainly been present before in Egypt, either as foreigners working in the country—often as mercenaries in the military—or as part of the Egyptian populace. Egypt, situated at the crossroads of Africa, the Near East, and the Aegean, was influenced by the infiltrations of people from abroad. What is more, the composition of the population of Nubia was not homogeneous and people of Nubian origin, just as people of Libyan origin, could hold important positions in Egypt. It is even possible that Egyptian royalty at times had some Nubian blood.

Despite some variation in facial types from period to period, both royal and private heads utilize certain forms which characterizes them as Egyptian, as distinguished from the Egyptian representations of foreigners. For example, the Libyan kings of Dynasties XXII–XXIV almost invariably have themselves portrayed in much the same manner as their Ramesside predecessors. The one glaring exception to this rule appears to be Cat. 89, a faience plaque bearing a relief representation of one of the kings of Dynasty XXIII named Iuput. Here, however, the King appears to have been represented not as a Libyan but as a Nubian. This figure's blunt nose and thick lips, its costume, its broad shoulders and low, narrow waist, are closely paralleled in certain royal reliefs of Dynasty XXV. Indeed, it is the close resemblance of this work to royal representations of Dynasty XXV which permits us to identify the king as Iuput II (731–720 B.C.) rather than Iuput I (804–783 B.C). Iuput I died before Kashta, the first Nubian king to invade Egypt, was born, while Iuput II was one of the rulers who surrendered and swore allegiance to Kashta's successor Piankhy, now known as Piye. Although there are no prototypes as yet found from either Egypt or the Sudan which could have served as a model for this relief plaque of Iuput, it seems reasonable to assume they once existed and that this piece reflects the new royal influence.

It has been suggested that the concept of portraying a king as of a given ethnic type was dependent ultimately upon the concept of individualistic representation first developed during Dynasty XII, beginning with Sesostris III (Cat. 40). Thus it is possible, especially since Nubian inscriptions employ Middle Kingdom language, that sculptures of that period may in some way have influenced Nubian royal art. In his time King Sesostris III may have proclaimed himself a god in the Sudan; he certainly was recognized as a god of the region in Egyptian temples of the New Kingdom and thus was claimed as an ancestor by the Nubian kings. It should also be noted that an archaizing style reflecting features of the Middle Kingdom as well as other periods began in the Third Intermediate Period, just prior to Dynasty XXV. Therefore, the archaizing trends in the art cannot be attributed solely to Nubian influence.

The art of the Nubian kings at Thebes was, except for facial features and some details of costume, more or less Egyptian in style. In Nubia, on the other hand, royal monuments of the period sometimes show interesting deviations from Egyptian forms. A few sculptures of Taharqa from the Upper Nile, for example, are of heavier build with more brutal features than those so far found in Egypt; perhaps, despite Egyptian influence, they represent a more Nubian approach to their subject. Something of this is to be seen in Taharqa's *shawabtis* (Cat. 92) which, even if fairly simple, seem to represent a realistically non-Egyptian physiognomy. And if reliefs in the Nubian temples often imitated Egyptian style and were done by Egyptian craftsmen, they sometimes exhibit a freshness of conception, free from the traditions of normal Egyptian temple iconography. Taharqa's temples at Sanam, opposite El Kurru, have scenes showing long processions of a type unparalleled in Egypt; and some of Piankhy's temple reliefs at nearby Gebel Barkal are more roughly carved, with lankier proportions, than contemporary reliefs in Egypt. Moreover, these scenes, which depict the capitulation of Piankhy's opponents, decorated a courtyard in which stood a stela commemorating Piankhy's victories leading up to and including this capitulation. And neither the stela nor the wall reliefs portray that event in quite the same manner as older Egyptian monuments of this genre. The stela is especially interesting, for its relief summarizes in a highly condensed manner the various stages in the surrender of Piankhy's opponents instead of rendering Piankhy in one of the symbolic poses of royal victory (Cat. 36b), as would probably have been true of the decoration of a stela commemorating the victories of an Egyptian pharaoh.

The rule of the Nubians helped bring about a rebirth of the arts. The country was prosperous and once again large royal building projects were undertaken. However, in this Dynasty there apparently was not the degree of influence of royal art upon private art as in former periods; and for this there are several reasons.

First, although the country was subject to the Nubians, the kings of Dynasty XXV generally resided at their native capital in the Sudan. Actual control of Egypt was placed in the hands of relatives appointed to a few key posts and local officials whose allegiance the kings accepted. Therefore there was by no means the degree of political unity which Egypt had enjoyed prior to the Third Intermediate Period, and there was thus still fertile soil in which local styles might continue to grow.

Secondly, the latter part of the XXVth Dynasty saw the Nubian kings at war with Assyria, and Egypt was invaded several times. During this time another dynasty rose to power at Sais, the old capital of the Western Delta in Dynasty XXIV. Eventually, when Thebes was sacked by the Assyrians and the last Nubian king driven back to his homeland, Egypt, now subject to Assyria, stood fragmented. The two major powers were Mentuemhat (Cat. 95 and 96), who governed Upper Egypt from Thebes, and Psamtik I of Dynasty XXVI, who controlled the North. In 656 B.C. the latter tended his kingdom to Upper Egypt and was recognized throughout the land.

There occurred an artistic renaissance in late Dynasty XXV and Dynasty XXVI as first the South under Mentuemhat and the North under Psamtik I, followed by an Egypt united under Psamtik, weathered the troubled times and emerged from Nubian control and Assyrian domination.

Evidence for this and the following decades of the Late Period in the Delta is scanty, and this is especially unfortunate because from now on the North was the true center of power in the country. But it is clear that large constructions were undertaken, and at Giza and Saqqara several well-decorated tombs of the reign of Psamtik I are still preserved. At Thebes Mentuemhat built the first of a series of monumental and lavishly appointed private tombs, while one official, the Vizier Nespekashuty, usurped a tomb of Dynasty XI and lined it with new reliefs. The plans for and many elements of the decoration of these new grand tombs were innovative, although in part they revived ancient forms of architectural embellishment while the reliefs which decorated them were to a great extent archaizing. Simple, staid compositions based on the Old Kingdom (Cat. 97b) stood directly next to more lively scenes reflecting the New Kingdom (Cat. 97a); and generally the decoration bears the stamp of the new formal elegance of the age (Cat. 96a).

Although monuments from other than Theban sites were utilized as prototypes, the major tombs of Thebes reflect an affinity felt with and a desire to recreate the grand past of that city. All these funerary monuments were in the cemetery below the temples of Mentuhotep II of Dynasty XI and Hatshepsut of Dynasty XVIII, reminders of two great past Theban ages. Reliefs from the temple of Hatshepsut were copied in several of the new tombs. In the North, on the other hand, the monuments used as models were most often those found in that region.

There were also major developments in private statuary as more sculptures were made. For a brief period of time in late Dynasty XXV and early Dynasty XXVI there appeared alongside more traditionally idealizing (Cat. 94) and archaizing statues, sculptures with more realistic faces (Cat. 93 and 95), sometimes brutally so. These physiognomies occasionally take their inspiration from the faces of Nubian royal sculptures; and one relief of King Psamtik I—almost certainly from Heliopolis—which portrays the King with a very realistic face, has a short, rounded skull strongly reminiscent of Nubian royalty. A major influence may also have been exercised by realistic faces of the late Middle Kingdom. Some statuary probably came from the North, as for example, Cat. 93; and, as archaizing works harking back to the realistic physiognomies of Dynasty XII are also known from that region, it is possible that the new realism was in part a local tradition not totally dependent upon a Nubian influence. As far as one can judge from the currently available evidence, pre-Dynasty XXV archaizing tendencies in the Third Intermediate Period first became prominent not at Thebes but in regions further to the North.

With the increase in power of Dynasty XXVI in all parts of the land, Egypt once again became a real political entity as Psamtik I and his successors placed their own men in key positions. Art flourished throughout the Nile Valley, and an archaizing style continued in use as if the Egyptians wanted to recreate the glories of yore. After the reign of Psamtik I, the realistic faces vanished from the statuary and private sculptures came to reflect the now prevailing idealization of faces in royal works.

How dramatic the artistic renaissance of Dynasty XXV and Dynasty XXVI was may be appreciated when one considers the state of the arts, especially the funerary arts, since the end of the Ramesside Period. Then the decline in royal power had a profound impact upon the arts, enhanced by the unsettled and economically unfavorable conditions of the time. As a result the Egyptians may have felt a greater sense of personal dependence on their gods, divorced from the state cults. Secular scenes vanished from the tomb walls, and tombs were eventually reduced to simple subterranean chambers.

The royal mummies of the New Kingdom, whose looting could no longer be prevented, were removed finally to a hidden tomb for safekeeping. In the same spirit unobtrusive communal burials became more common for private people, and at Thebes many were buried in grounds of royal temples which were more easily protected. As if in compensation for the lost tomb decoration, the coffins came to be adorned with numerous small scenes showing the deceased offering to the gods and protected by the deity and divine symbols. This kind of decoration, with its love of intricate patterns, remained common throughout the Late Period (Cat. 102).

The decoration of funerary stelae also underwent changes

reflecting a greater dependence upon the gods for survival in the next life rather than upon the funerary cult observed by the relatives and friends of the deceased. Although stelae of similar format were known earlier, by the Third Intermediate Period most stelae came to conform to a similar iconographical pattern. The upper part of the stela was round-topped and decorated with symbols of the gods, especially the solar disk under a hieroglyph for heaven. Below were scenes of the deceased with the gods, while at the very bottom came an inscription invoking the god's blessings (Cat. 100). This type of stela continued throughout the Late Period even though chronological and regional variations in style and content can be discerned.

The composition of Cat. 101, for example, associating the deceased with the solar cycle of birth, death, and rebirth, seems to have been characteristic of the site of Akhmim, in Middle Egypt. Its style too differs from that of Cat. 100. Even though regional variations in art exist throughout the Late Period, certain features are found at several sites, especially after Dynasty XXV when the country achieved a greater degree of political unity. On Cat. 101 and 109, for example, made two hundred or more years apart, the deceased wear the same kind of long skirt suspended by a single strap and have similar high, rounded skulls with small faces.

In the Third Intermediate Period, as tomb decoration lost significance, the making of tomb sculptures was almost discontinued. As in the Ramesside Period, the temple sculptures came to show figures holding divine symbols as well as figures of the gods. In fact, private persons now dedicated statues of gods with inscriptions invoking them to grant life to the donors.

It was thus a great break with tradition when in late Dynasty XXV and Dynasty XXVI new tombs were constructed which were painted with religious scenes. Others were decorated with scenes of daily life (Cat. 96a) as well as with representations of funerary offerings for the dead (Cat. 97b). It was also a break with tradition that in several tombs the old custom of cutting sculptures of the deceased and his wife from the living rock was briefly revived. Other elements of the decoration remained more within current traditions of funerary art; but even these could at the same time show archaizing tendencies. For example, although the female mourners of Nespekashuty were most probably inspired by the treatment of this subject in a New Kingdom tomb, this motif of mourning women had continued to be represented on coffins after the decoration of tombs had all but ceased. Also, the guardian genii of Mentuemhat (Cat. 95), although used as tomb sculptures, are simply three-dimensional versions of protective deities known also from coffins of the Third Intermediate and Late Periods. But this renaissance was limited in its scope and duration. Most burials throughout the Late Period were quite simple; only burial equipment such as coffins bore decoration.

When Dynasty XXX ushered in a strong period of native rule the arts, as in Dynasty XXVI, flourished. Although traditional forms were maintained, there were strong archaizing tendencies. This time, however, the approach was less eclectic; the model to be emulated was the art of Dynasty XXVI (Cat. 103). Equally important is the fact that, beginning with Dynasty XXVII, true portraits appear in sculpture in the round which go far beyond the realistic faces fashioned in Dynasty XXV and early Dynasty XXVI. This trend continues through Dynasty XXX (Cat. 104) and the entire Ptolemaic Period.

Egypt's conquest by Alexander and the rule of the Ptolemies brought about a cross-fertilization of Egyptian and Hellenistic art but gradually undermined Pharaonic civilization. Native Egyptian culture, however, did not die out until Christian times, for the Ptolemies, unlike the Romans after them, governed the country as resident pharaohs. Egyptian temples were built throughout the land and in parts of Nubia, and these temples were of traditional construction and their decoration maintained and elaborated upon traditional forms (Cat. 106 and 107). After the fifth century B.C. both relief and statuary (Cat. 113 and 114) often show a greater fullness and plasticity of form than in previous ages, but there are precedents for such features in the earlier part of the Late Period; from it stems much of Egyptian art of the Ptolemaic Period.

Outside the temples the world was gradually changing, as old burial customs gave way. But within the realm of temple statuary traditional forms such as block statues (Cat. 108) were maintained; and idealizing benign faces such as Cat. 105 and 108 in the Ptolemaic Period follow a prototype of Dynasty XXX (Cat. 103). The modeling of individualistic faces which may be considered to be true portraits began to show a more organic and integrated treatment of the head as a whole. If they also display a certain simplification and stylization of features, that is merely an indication that the new realism went hand in hand with yet another basic and still living ancient Egyptian tradition—traditions that would be maintained until the Roman conquest destroyed the class of noblemen and priests who supported this art.

Cat. 90. Head of a king. The sculptures of the Egyptianized Nubian conquerors of Egypt, although executed in both traditional and archaizing Egyptian forms, also reveal the non-Egyptian side of their heritage. That this head represents such a conqueror, probably King Shabako, is confirmed by the round skull, thick neck, double uraeus, skullcap with band, and the roughening of the upper surfaces to receive gilding. Dynasty XXV. Green slate. Height 7.1 cm.

90

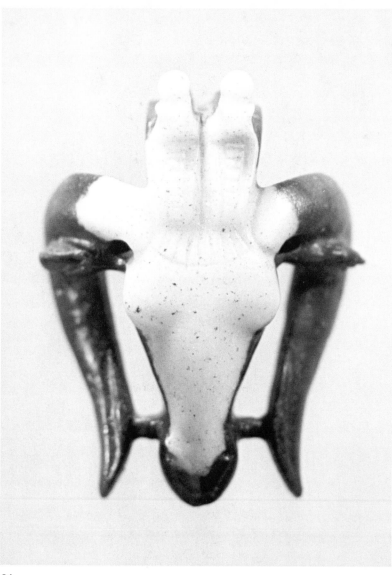

91

Cat. 91. Ram's head amulet. This piece has a loop for suspension in the rear. It was carved so that the stone's banding conforms to the natural divisions between face and horns. The ram was a symbol of Amun, chief deity of the Nubians. This type of amuletic earring or necklace pendant, here with solar disk and double uraeus, was an innovation of Dynasty XXV. Green and white jasper. Height 3.9 cm.

Cat. 92. Mummiform *shawabti* of King Taharqa holding hoes. Among the Egyptian burial customs adopted by the Nubian kings of Dynasty XXV was the use of *shawabtis*: figures believed to perform magically work required of their owner in the hereafter. King Taharqa of late Dynasty XXV had over one thousand of them. Some, such as this with its high skull, broad nose and face, and small mouth with heavy lips, reflect the style of certain major sculptures of their time. Magnesite marble. Height 40.2 cm.

Cat. 93a-b. Bust of a man. The art of the Late Period, a time of much political fragmentation, is characterized by the coexistence of a number of styles. This bust, with its prominent shoulder blades, high cheek bones, and receding forehead, has a somewhat foreign physiognomy, perhaps Libyan, and a realism known from a number of sculptures of early Dynasty XXVI with which it must be contemporary. Gray black basalt. Height 11.0 cm.

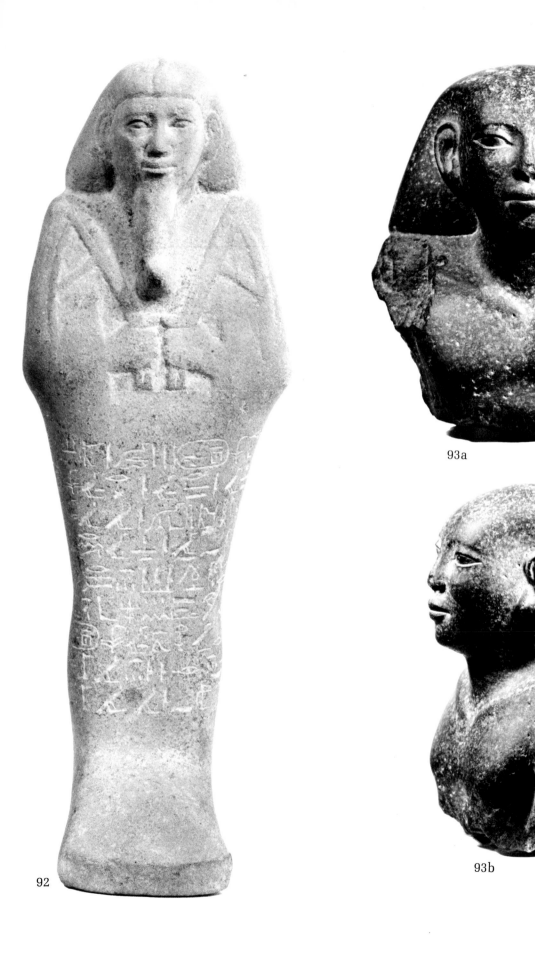

92

93a

93b

Cat. 94. Block statue of Pedi-mahes. It is dated to late Dynasty XXV by stylistic elements such as lack of a connection between chin and block, limbs half in the round, and the short garment which leaves the feet uncovered. Nearly contemporary with Cat. 93, to which it is related by its raised head, this sculpture, whose inscriptions link it to the Delta, was executed in a more traditionally idealizing fashion. Gray granite. Height 46.3 cm.

94

Cat. 95. Guardians of Mentuemhat. Among the works created for this late Dynasty XXV and early Dynasty XXVI official was a group of sculptures of deities of a type otherwise known only in reliefs and paintings. Imsety (Cat. 79), holding lizards, and Hapy, holding a snake, are invoked to stand eternal vigil over their owner. They are probably from his tomb's burial chamber. Black diorite. Height 51.0 cm.

95

96a

Cat. 96a-c. Relief from the tomb of Mentuemhat. An important power in Upper Egypt during late Dynasty XXV and early Dynasty XXVI, Mentuemhat, Count of Thebes commanded a splendid tomb. Its decoration, elements of which are unique (Cat. 95), was executed in several styles, one of which, represented by this relief, was archaizing. These scenes of a woman pulling a thorn from a companion's foot and a woman with a child stacking fruit were inspired by small but unusual details in the paintings of a nearby Dynasty XVIII tomb (Cat. 96b-c, not in exhibition). The discerning eye which admired these paintings did not merely copy. In the original the two scenes were not juxtaposed nor was the woman neatly framed by trees. In keeping with this eclectic sophistication, everything, including the new, elaborate wigs and lotus-legged chair, is imbued with greater elegance. Limestone. Height 23.9 cm.

96b

96c

97a

Cat. 97a-b. Funeral ceremonies for
Nespekashuty. The decoration of
this Vizier's tomb, though somewhat less elegant and carefully
carved, resembles reliefs from the
tomb of his contemporary, Mentuemhat (Cat. 96a). These mourners
with emotionless faces and agitated
gestures (not an unusual combination in Egyptian art) are based on
Dynasty XVIII prototypes; but as
animated, buxom mourners appear
on coffins of the immediately preceding periods, they may also represent a living tradition. The lower
portion of a part of this procession
included squatting and prostrate
figures and stood above a file of
female offering bearers (Cat. 97b,
not in exhibition) basically of Old
Kingdom type. Similar female
bearers, one in the M. H. de Young
Memorial Museum, are known from
the tomb of Mentuemhat. Early
Dynasty XXVI. Limestone. Height
34.5 cm.

97b

98b

98a

99

Cat. 98a-b. King Necho II kneeling. Probably this statuette was originally part of a votive group showing the King offering to a god. The figure differs from the only other similar bronze representation of this King in its broader headcloth, facial features, and horizontal tripartition (rather than the traditional vertical bipartition) of the torso. This latter sculptural convention was soon to become popular. Dynasty XXVI. Bronze. Height 13.6 cm.

Cat. 99. The god Horus. Bronze, inlaid with gold. The falcon wears the Double Crown of Upper and Lower Egypt (see Fig. 12 and Cat. 35, left, respectively), indicative of his role as divine king. The figure was originally part of a falcon's coffin or other votive offering. Bronzes of deities, difficult to date (Cat. 87), are common in the Late Period. Dynasty XXVI or later. Height 28.8 cm.

Cat. 100. Stela of Iret-horru. Beneath heaven (symbolized by the stela's rounded top) and the winged sun supported by *was*-scepters, Iret-horru, priest of Amun, worships a mummiform Osiris and his wife Isis. The inscription invokes Osiris' blessings. The main aesthetic device, the contrast of roughened light areas against the darker polished field, was also employed in other periods, but details of style and texts make an attribution to Dynasty XXV possible. Black stone. Height 50.8 cm.

100

101

102

Cat. 101. Stela of Hordyef-nakht. The decoration represents the solar cycle associated with the life, death, and rebirth of Hordyef-nakht. In the second register, beneath the solar disk in heaven, the sun rises (left) and the solar boat enters the west (right) bearing Hordyef-nakht adoring figures of the rising, risen, and setting sun. Below is represented simultaneously the sun's reception into, and departure from, the underworld, commencing a new cycle. Probably Dynasty XXX. Limestone. Height 75.5 cm.

Cat. 102. Cartonnage of Neskhonsu-pakhered, Mistress of the House and Songstress of Amun. From the late New Kingdom on, while tomb decoration declined, coffins became more elaborately decorated with many motifs including protective deities. In the guise of Osiris, Neskhonsu-pakhered, wearing a wig with vulture headdress, is guarded by a winged ram's head of Amun-Re, the Four Sons of Horus, a Horus falcon, Isis and Nephthys flanking an Osiride emblem, and two more falcons. Dynasties XXV-XXVI. Length 173.0 cm.

Cat. 103a-b. Statue of a priest of Amun. The Late Period witnessed successive attempts to recapture past glory. For Dynasty XXX, the "good old days" were Dynasty XXVI; and this sculpture of Dynasty XXX is based upon works of the XXVIth Dynasty, themselves inspired by Old Kingdom monuments (Cat. 23 and 25). But it is not a copy. It is linked to art from Dynasty XXVI on by its wig, and the division of the torso into three horizontal segments (Cat. 98), despite the faint median line. It is also related to sculpture of its own time and later by the representation of gods on the back pillar, the idealized, smiling face, and its highly polished, swelling forms. Black diorite. Height 51.2 cm.

103a

103b

104c

Cat. 104a-c. Head of Wesir-wer. Cat. 104c shows the head reunited with its body (Egyptian Museum, Cairo, not in exhibition). In contrast to the archaizing and idealizing tendencies of some contemporary works (Cat. 103), this sculpture shows a garment of its own time and represents a new trend in Late Period art: the creation of heads with sufficient individuality and expression to warrant the label of portrait. The eyes are traditional; nose, mouth, and skull shape are not. Individuality does not, however, extend to the figures of the three deities held. The Osiris (*Wesir*) and bird (*wer*, i.e. "great") on the top of the back pillar (Cat. 104b) are simultaneously a representation of the god, a statement that he is great, and a rebus of the priest's name. Dynasty XXX. Green slate. Height of head 15.3 cm.

104b

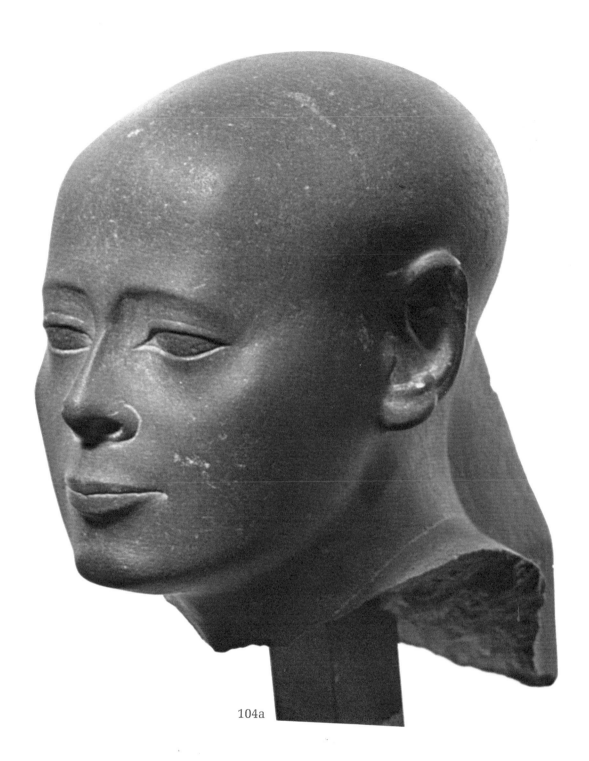

104a

105

Cat. 105. Royal bust. The king represented may be identified as Ptolemy II on the basis of inscribed sculptures of that King whose facial features display the same variations of an ideal type known from earlier times (Cat. 103). Sculptures of parts of the human or animal body, of which this is an uncommonly large specimen, have been identified as sculptors' models and votive offerings. Some of these sculptures may have been both. Many artists were temple personnel, and a sculpture, even if made as a model could also at some point be used as an actual offering. It is also possible that the very creation of a sculpture might have been considered an offering to the gods. Ptolemaic Period. Limestone. Height 45.0 cm.

Cat. 106. King presenting an offering. The general style and such details as the slightly puffy face and subdued tripartition of the torso suggest this work was carved for Ptolemy II at the temple of Isis at Behbeit el Higara under the influence of the Dynasty XXX reliefs there. Behind him, in another scene, is a figure of a goddess. Ptolemaic Period. Red and black granite. Height 69.0 cm.

Cat. 107. Sunk relief of king offering an image of Maat. The dramatic difference in style between this relief and Cat. 106 is due in part to its being several centuries later in time. But the difference is also due to its being from an Egyptian temple in Nubia, far from the main artistic centers, where it was carved in the friable sandstone of that region. Both its subject matter and the pose of the figure testify to the remarkable continuity of temple iconography in ancient Egypt (Cat. 77 and 106). The king is shown offering an image of Maat, the divine order of the universe in the form of a goddess, to a now lost representation of a deity or deities. Late Ptolemaic or early Roman Period. Sandstone. Height 48.5 cm.

106

107

108a

108b

Cat. 108a-b. Nes-Thoth, Craftsman of Amun, son of Pediwesir. The figure of an ape (Thoth) on his robe may symbolize his devotion to his divine namesake. This Ptolemaic sculpture has facial features similar to Cat. 103, 105, and 106, and a tall, shallow head and body, common to Ptolemaic block statues. Private sculptures seldom hold *ankh*-signs, generally a prerogative of gods and kings. The presence of these signs on a few Ptolemaic block statues associated with Osiris (Cat. 41) may be explained by analogy with certain paintings in magical papyri, where *ankh*-signs are held by figures of the deceased at the moment of rebirth. Third or second century B.C. Black diorite. Height 39.0 cm.

Cat. 109. Stela of Pakhaes. Beneath the vault of heaven, the solar disk, and two jackals, the deceased is sitting with his mother behind him. On his knees is perched oddly a figure of Osiris. Before him his dutiful son offers him incense and a libation. The stela is datable, on the basis of its style and inscriptions, to approximately 150 to 75 B.C. The family represented is known from two other monuments and held titles relating its members to Medinet Habu and the Theban Necropolis. Limestone, painted and gilded. Height 37.5 cm.

109

110

111

112

Cat. 110. *Ba*-bird amulet. The human-headed bird, the *Ba,* represented one of the forms of life after death in which the Egyptians believed (Fig. 8). Ptolemaic Period. Gold, inlaid with lapis lazuli, turquoise, and steatite. Width 7.0 cm.

Cat. 111. Winged scarab beetle. Symbol of the rising sun and ever renewing life, the scarab attached to a mummy became the heart which would not testify against the deceased at his final judgment. Late Period. Faience glazed in two shades of blue. Total width 25.5 cm.

Cat. 112. Terminal from a broad collar necklace. Necklaces with falcon-headed terminals were represented in reliefs from the Old Kingdom onward; actual examples exist as early as the Middle Kingdom. Labeled in certain texts as the "collar of Horus," such necklaces afforded magical protection for their wearers (Cat. 73). The twisted gold wire and fused multicolored glass inlay indicate the piece was made during the Ptolemaic Period. Opaque red, white, blue, yellow, and black glass fused together and set into a gold mounting. Height 3.0 cm.

Cat. 113a-b. Queen or goddess holding a floral scepter. Although apparently nude, this torso actually wears a clinging garment. The full, sensuous forms are Ptolemaic; however, excluding the Amarna Period (Cat. 60), female figures somewhat similarly treated are known from the late New Kingdom. This piece was made during the first half of the third century B.C. Pale green glassy faience. Height 10.6 cm.

Cat. 114. Stela of Horus-on-the-Crocodiles. The child god is represented dominating scorpions, serpents, oryx, lion, and crocodiles. These figures and the texts and other representations of deities which cover the stela make it a magical protection against and cure for the ravages of the creatures represented. Himself once cured, Horus is conjured to save the petitioner who, by drinking water poured over the monuments, could swallow the magic absorbed from both texts and representations. Objects of this type occurred in Ramesside times, were very rare in Dynasty XXVI, and were most popular during the fourth and third centuries B.C. This piece probably dates from the third century B.C. Black steatite. Height 23.2 cm.

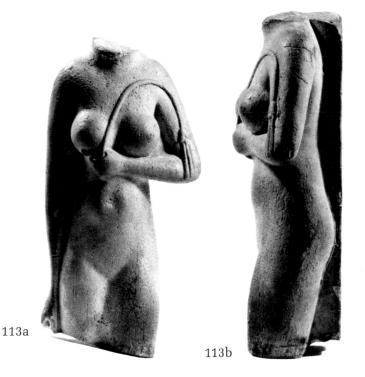

113a

113b

114

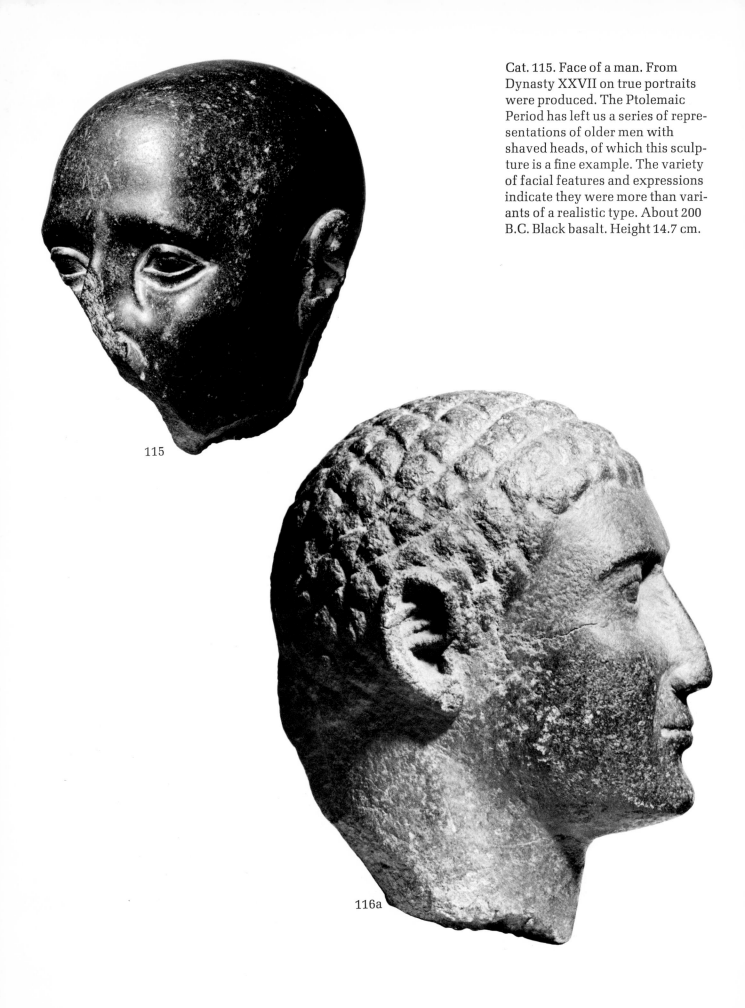

115

116a

Cat. 115. Face of a man. From Dynasty XXVII on true portraits were produced. The Ptolemaic Period has left us a series of representations of older men with shaved heads, of which this sculpture is a fine example. The variety of facial features and expressions indicate they were more than variants of a realistic type. About 200 B.C. Black basalt. Height 14.7 cm.

Cat. 116a-b. Head of a man. During the second and first centuries B.C. a number of sculptures were produced in which the Egyptian treatment of the faces as relatively simplified forms contrasts with the curly Hellenistic coiffures. This head, although more simply modeled than some, has sufficient individuality to demonstrate that it portrayed to some extent the actual physiognomy of the official for whom it was made. About 80 to 40 B.C. Dark basalt. Height 31.8 cm.

116b

117a

Cat. 117a-b. The Brooklyn "Black Head." Because of the strong difference in color of the polished and unpolished surfaces, this head displays an even greater contrast between its Egyptian face and Hellenistic coiffure than does Cat. 116. Like that piece, this sculpture demonstrates a contemporary interaction between Egyptian art and art from other parts of the Hellenistic world, and also continues both a native idealizing tradition nearly three thousand years old and a more recent native tradition of portaiture. In its colossal scale and superb craftsmanship it represents the final flowering of Egyptian sculpture in the round before the Roman conquest brought about its rapid decline. About 80 to 50 B.C. Diorite. Height 41.4 cm.

117b

Bibliography and Abbreviations

Aldred 1973:
Aldred, C. A., *Akhenaten and Nefertiti.*
(Brooklyn, 1973)

Brooklyn 1952:
*Egyptian Art in The Brooklyn Museum
Collection.* (Brooklyn, 1952)

Brooklyn 1956:
The Brooklyn Museum. *Five Years of
Collecting Egyptian Art, 1951-1956.
Catalogue of an Exhibition Held at The
Brooklyn Museum 11 December, 1956 to
17 March, 1957.* (Brooklyn, 1956. Reprinted
1969)

Brooklyn 1968:
*Ancient Egyptian Glass and Glazes in
The Brooklyn Museum.* By Elizabeth
Riefstahl. Wilbour Monographs–I.
(Brooklyn, 1968)

Brooklyn 1974a:
*Corpus of Hieroglyphic Inscriptions in
The Brooklyn Museum. Vol. I. From
Dynasty I to the End of Dynasty XVIII.*
By T. G. H. James. Wilbour Monographs–
VI. (Brooklyn, 1974)

Brooklyn 1974b:
The Brooklyn Museum. *Brief Guide to
the Department of Egyptian and Classical
Art.* By B. V. Bothmer and J. L. Keith.
(Brooklyn, 1974)

California 1927:
Lutz, H. F., *Egyptian Tomb Steles and
Offering Stones of the Museum of Anthro-
pology and Ethnology of the University
of California.* University of California
Publications in Egyptian Archaeology,
IV. (Leipzig, 1927)

California 1930:
Lutz, H. F., *Egyptian Statues and Statu-
ettes in the Museum of Anthropology of
the University of California.* University
of California Publications in Egyptian
Archaeology, V. (Leipzig, 1930)

California 1932:
Reisner, G. A., *A Provincial Cemetery of
the Pyramid Age. Naga-ed-Dêr.* Pt. III.
University of California Publications in
Egyptian Archaeology, VI. (Oxford, 1932)

California 1965:
Lythgoe, A.M., *The Predynastic Cemetery
N 7000. Naga-ed-Dêr.* Pt. IV. Edited by
D. Dunham. University of California Pub-
lications in Egyptian Archaeology, VII.
(Berkeley and Los Angeles, 1965)

California 1966:
Berkeley, University of California.
*Ancient Egypt: An Exhibition at the
Robert H. Lowie Museum of Anthro-
pology of the University of California,
Berkeley, March 25–October 23, 1966.*
(The Regents of the University of Cali-
fornia, 1966)

California 1968:
Berkeley, University of California.
*Treasurers of the Lowie Museum. An
Exhibition of the Robert H. Lowie
Museum of Anthropology, University of
California, Berkeley, January 2–October
27, 1968* (University of California, 1968)

Cooney 1965:
Cooney, J.D., *Amarna Reliefs from
Hermopolis in American Collections.*
(Brooklyn, 1965)

Porter and Moss 1974:
Porter, B., and Moss, R., assisted by
Burney, E., *Topographical Bibliography
of Ancient Egyptian Hieroglyphic Texts,
Reliefs, and Paintings. Vol. 3, pt. 2, Abú
Rawâsh to Abûsir.* 2nd ed., rev. and aug.
by J. Málek. (Oxford, 1974)

Roeder 1969:
Roeder, G., *Amarna-Reliefs aus Hermopolis. Ausgrabungen der Deutschen
Hermopolis-Expedition in Hermopolis
1929-1939.* Vol. 2. Edited by R. Hanke.
Hildesheim, Pelizaeus-Museum. Wissen-
schaftliche Veröffentlichung, 6. (Hildesheim, 1969)

Vandier 1958:
Vandier, J., *Manuel d'archéologie
égyptienne. Vol. 3, Les grandes époques;
la statuaire.* (Paris, 1958)

Concordance I

Catalogue numbers : Accession numbers;
provenance, measurements, bibliography.

Cat. 1: Brooklyn 07.447.502. El Ma'mariya, Tomb 2. Height 33.8 cm.; width across arms 11.0 cm.; depth 4.6 cm. *Bibl.*: Ucko, P. J., *Anthropomorphic Figurines of Predynastic Egypt* . . . (London, 1968), no. 73, p. 48, fig. 48 and p. 101.

Cat. 2: Lowie 6-3586. Naga ed-Deir, Grave N 7400. Height 24.5 cm.; greatest width 14.1 cm. *Bibl.*: California 1965, p. 242.

Cat. 3: Lowie 6-17633. El Ahaiwah, Tomb A 76. Height 25.2 cm.; diameter of rim 8.6 cm. *Bibl.*: California 1966, p. 27, illus.

Cat. 4: Lowie 6-4735. Naga ed-Deir, Grave N 7006. Height 7.9 cm.; width 15.6 cm. *Bibl.*: California 1966, p. 18, illus. For Grave N 7006 see, California 1965, p. 4.

Cat. 5: Lowie 6-3329. Naga ed-Deir, Grave N 7266. Height 12.0 cm.; greatest diameter 18.0 cm.; diameter of lip 8.0 cm. *Bibl.*: California 1965, pp. 151-153 and fig. 66; California 1966, pp. 24-25, illus.

Cat. 6: Lowie 6-4015. Naga ed-Deir, Grave N 7522. Height 23.0 cm.; greatest diameter 23.0 cm.; diameter of lip 12.0 cm. *Bibl.*: California 1965, p. 335, no. 10, p. 334, figs. 149a,b and p. 336, figs. 150a,e,f.; California 1966, p. 25, illus.; California 1968, p. 81, illus.

Cat. 7: Lowie 6-17557. El Ahaiwah, Tomb A 57. Length 18.1 cm.; width 7.0 cm. Bibl.: California 1966, p. 17, illus.

Cat. 8: Lowie 6-22233. Naga ed-Deir, Grave N 7304. Length 16.0 cm. *Bibl.*: California 1965, p. 180, no. 25a, p. 181, figs. 78a,c,d and p. 182, fig. 79d.

Cat. 9: Lowie 6-17171. Naga ed-Deir, Grave N 7304. Length 9.2 cm. *Bibl.*: California 1965, p. 179, no. 18, p. 181, figs. 78a,e,g and p. 182, fig. 79a; California 1966, p. 28, illus.

Cat. 10: Lowie 6-19071. El Ahaiwah, Tomb A 226. Height 17.0 cm.; length 40.0 cm. *Bibl.*: Smith, W. S., *The Art and Architecture of Ancient Egypt* (Baltimore, 1958), pp. 12-13 and pl. 3; California 1966, p. 24, illus.; California 1968, p. 84, illus.

Cat. 11: Brooklyn 73.26. Said to be from between Sohag and Baliana. Height 24.8 cm.; width 20.0 cm.; depth 33.1 cm. *Bibl.*: *The Brooklyn Museum Annual XIV, 1972-1973* (Brooklyn, 1974), p. 12. To be published by Y. Margowsky whose comments upon this piece are gratefully acknowledged.

Cat. 12: Brooklyn 58.192. Saqqara. Height 21.4 cm.; width 9.7 cm.; depth 8.7 cm.; height of face 2.1 cm. *Bibl.*: Wildung, D., *Miscellanea Wilbouriana* 1 (Brooklyn, 1972), pp. 145-160, figs. 6-10; Brooklyn 1974b, pp. 24-25, illus.

Cat. 13: Lowie 6-19784. Giza, Tomb G. 1024. Greatest diameter 20.0 cm. *Bibl.*: California 1966, p. 32, illus.; Reisner, G. A., *A History of the Giza Necropolis* II, ed. by W. S. Smith (Cambridge, Mass., 1955), p. 101, fig. 147 and pl. 45a,b.

Cat. 14: Lowie 6-22883. Naga ed-Deir, Tomb N 524. Length as reconstructed 28.0 cm. *Bibl.*: California 1932, pp. 88, 198-199 and pl. 39.

Cat. 15a: Brooklyn 46.167. Height 54.3 cm.; width 29.0 cm.; depth 32.0 cm.; height of face 18.2 cm. *Bibl.*: Cooney, J. D., *The Brooklyn Museum Bulletin 9*, no. 3 (Spring, 1948), pp. 1-12, illus.; Brooklyn 1974b, pp. 22-23, illus.

Cat. 15b: Plaster cast of Cat. 15a.

Cat. 16: Brooklyn 68.152. Height 17.0 cm.; width 18.0 cm.; depth 15.0 cm. *Bibl.*: Hempstead, New York, Hofstra University, Emily Lowe Gallery. *Art of Ancient Egypt; A Selection from The Brooklyn Museum . . . February 22 through April 6, 1971* (Hempstead, 1971), no. 1, illus.

Cat. 17: Lowie 6-19825. Giza, Tomb G 1201. Height 44.8 cm.; width 67.8 cm.; depth 7.6 cm. *Bibl.*: California 1927, pp. 1, 15 and pl. 1; California 1966, pp. 42-43, illus.; California 1968, p. 85, illus.; Porter and Moss 1974, p. 57.

Cat. 18: Brooklyn 72.58. Height 34.0 cm.; width 16.2 cm.; depth 12.8 cm.; height of face 6.9 cm. *Bibl.*: *The Brooklyn Museum Annual XIV, 1972-1973* (Brooklyn, 1974), p. 12.

Cat. 19: Brooklyn 39.119. Height 39.2 cm.; width 17.8 cm.; depth 24.9 cm.; height of queen's face 4.1 cm.; height of king's face 2.0 cm. *Bibl.*: Brooklyn 1952, no. 19, illus.; Brooklyn 1974a, no. 68, p. 28 and pls. IV, XXV; Brooklyn 1974b, pp. 30-31, illus.

Cat. 20a: Brooklyn 37.25E. Saqqara, Tomb D. 43. Height 42.6 cm.; width 74.4 cm.; depth 9.5 cm. *Bibl.*: Brooklyn 1952, no. 14, illus.; Smith, W. S., *A History of Egyptian Sculpture and Painting in the Old Kingdom*, 2nd. ed. (London, 1949), pp. 196, 304 and pl. 48; Brooklyn 1974a, no. 37, p. 14 and pl. XIX.

Cat. 20b: Drawing of a relief in the tomb of Seshemnofer IV at Giza (Tomb LG 53). After Junker, H. *Giza* XI (Vienna, 1953), fig. 89, p. 226. Courtesy Oesterreichische Akademie der Wissenschaften.

Cat. 21: Lowie 6-19770. Giza, Tomb G 1214. Height 36.0 cm. *Bibl.*: California 1930, p. 12 and pl. 18; Vandier 1958, p. 65; California 1966, p. 53, illus.; Porter and Moss 1974, p. 58.

Cat. 22: Lowie 6-19772. Giza, Tomb 1214. Height 40.0 cm. *Bibl.*: California 1930, pp. 18-19 and pls. 28b, 29a; Vandier 1958, p. 133; California 1966, p. 34, illus.; Porter and Moss 1974, p. 58.

Cat. 23: Lowie 6-19760. Giza, Tomb G 1020. Height 42.0 cm. *Bibl.*: California 1930, pp. 20-21 and pl. 32; Vandier 1958, pp. 79, 133; California 1966, p. 55, illus.; Porter and Moss 1974, p. 53.

Cat. 24: Lowie 6-19775. Giza, Tomb G 1206. Height 73.0 cm.; height of back slab 71.5 cm.; width of base 33.5 cm.; depth of base 25.0 cm. *Bibl.*: California 1930, pp. 22-24 and pls. 34, 35a,; Vandier 1958, p. 74 and pl. XXV, 4; California 1966, p. 41, illus.; Porter and Moss 1974, p. 58.

Cat. 25: Brooklyn 37.17E. Saqqara. Height 73.5 cm.; width 25.0 cm.; depth 20.8 cm.; height of man's face 7.3 cm.; height of wife's face 3.1 cm.; height of son's face 3.1 cm. Bibl.: Cooney, J. D., The Brooklyn Museum Bulletin 13, no. 3 (Spring, 1952), pp. 11-15, figs. 5-6; Vandier 1958, p. 77 and pl. XXV.

Cat. 26a-b: Lowie 6-19768. Giza, Tomb G 1152. Height 44.0 cm. Bibl.: California 1930, p. 27 and pls. 39-40; Vandier 1958, pp. 91, 140 and pl. XXXV, 3-4; California 1966, p. 36, illus.; California 1968, p. 83, illus.; Porter and Moss 1974, p. 56.

Cat. 27: Lowie 6-19766. Giza, Tomb G 1213. Height 18.5 cm.; width 12.0 cm.; depth 34.0 cm. Bibl.: California 1930, p. 28 and pl. 41b; California 1966, p. 39, illus.; Porter and Moss 1974, p. 58.

Cat. 28: Lowie 6-15215. Naga ed-Deir, unnumbered tomb group. Height 40.5 cm. Bibl.: California 1966, p. 60, illus.; presumably one of the sculptures in Reisner, G. A., Annales du Service des Antiquités de l'Egypte 5 (1904), pl. V, 1.

Cat. 29: Lowie 6-16024. Naga ed-Deir, no tomb number. Height 43.6 cm.; width 55.0 cm.; depth 5.0 cm. Bibl.: none. This piece differs in style from the other stelae published from Naga ed-Deir.

Cat. 30: Lowie 6-1903. Naga ed-Deir, Tomb N 3804. Height 65.0 cm.; width 62.0 cm.; depth 12.0 cm. Bibl.: Dunham, D., Naga-ed-Dêr Stelae of the First Intermediate Period (Boston, 1937), no. 71, pp. 83, 84, 122 and 124, and pls. I, 3, XXV; Schenkel, W., Frühmittelaegyptische Studien (Bonn, 1962, p. 99; Schenkel, W., Memphis. Herakleopolis. Theben. . . . Aegyptologische Abhandlungen 12 (Wiesbaden, 1965), no. 232, pp. 171-172; California 1966, p. 62, illus.

Cat. 31: Lowie 6-19881. Naga ed-Deir, no tomb number. Height 65.2 cm.; width 38.5 cm.; depth 10.0 cm. Bibl.: California 1927, no. 28, pp. 3, 16 and pl. 15; Dunham, D., Naga-ed-Dêr Stelae of the First Intermediate Period (Boston, 1937), no. 31, pp. 44, 45, 124; Schenkel, W., Frühmittelaegyptische Studien (Bonn, 1962), p. 101; Schenkel, W., Memphis. Herakleopolis. Theben. . . . Aegyptologische Abhandlungen 12 (Wiesbaden, 1965), no. 300, pp. 198-199.

Cat. 32: Brooklyn 51.231. Thebes, Deir el Bahri, Tomb 311. Height 13.2 cm.; width 24.5 cm. Bibl.: Riefstahl, E., Journal of Near Eastern Studies 15 (1956), pp. 10-17 and pls. VIII, X; Brooklyn 1956, no. 27b, pp. 24-25 and pl. 46; Brooklyn 1974a, no. 83, pp. 35-36 and pl. XXX.

Cat. 33a: Brooklyn 54.49. Thebes, Deir el Bahri, Tomb 311. Height 19.0 cm.; width 23.6 cm.; depth 1.9 cm. Bibl.: Riefstahl, E., Journal of Near Eastern Studies 15 (1956), pp. 10-17 and pls. IX-X; Brooklyn 1956, no. 27a, pp. 24-25 and pl. 47; Brooklyn 1974a, no. 82, p. 35 and pl. XXX; Brooklyn 1974b, pp. 32-33, illus.

Cat. 33b: After Riefstahl, E., Journal of Near Eastern Studies 15 (1956), pl. X. See also Vandier, J., Manuel d'archéologie égyptienne. Vol. 4, Bas reliefs et peintures (Paris, 1964), p. 173, fig. 63.

Cat. 34: Lowie 6-19870. Deir el Ballas. Height 68.0 cm.; width 99.0 cm.; depth 12.0 cm. Bibl.: California 1927, no. 64, pp. 6, 20 and pl. 33; Fischer, H. G., Inscriptions from the Coptite Nome. . . . Analecta Orientalia, 40 (Rome, 1964), no. 47, pp. 103, 119-120 and pl. XXXIX.

Cat. 35: Brooklyn 37.16E. Armant. Height 80.1 cm.; width 135.0 cm.; depth 11.5 cm.; height of faces 6.8 cm. Bibl.: Brooklyn 1952, no. 26, illus.; Aldred, C., Metropolitan Museum Journal 3 (1970), pp. 31-33; Brooklyn 1974a, no. 84, pp. 36-37 and pls. V, XXXI.

Cat. 36a: Brooklyn 52.129. Lisht, funerary temple of King Sesostris I. Height 52.5 cm.; width 59.0 cm.; depth 13.5 cm. Bibl.: Hayes, W. C., The Scepter of Egypt; A Background for the Study of the Egyptian Antiquities in the Metropolitan Museum of Art, Vol. I (New York, 1953), p. 188-189 and fig. 115; Brooklyn 1956, no. 28, p. 25; Brooklyn 1974a, no. 92, p. 40 and pl. XXXII.

Cat. 36b: Reconstruction of a scene in the funerary temple of King Pepy II at Saqqara. After Jéquier, G., Le monument funéraire de Pepi II, vol. II (Cairo, 1938), pl. 36.

Cat. 37: Brooklyn 52.130.2:. Lisht. Height 45.8 cm.; width 23.3 cm.; depth 5.9 cm. Bibl.: Brooklyn 1956, no. 25, pp. 22-23 and pl. 45.

Cat. 38: Brooklyn 59.1. Height 23.6 cm.; width 15.5 cm.; depth 10.6 cm.; height of face 5.6 cm. Bibl.: Brooklyn 1974b, pp. 36-37, illus.

Cat. 39: Brooklyn 56.85. Height 38.9 cm.; width 34.9 cm.; depth 36.7 cm.; height of face 20.2 cm. Bibl.: Brooklyn 1956, no. 2, p. 3 and pls. 7-10; Vandier 1958, pp. 224, 257; Roullet, A., The Egyptian and Egyptianizing Monuments of Imperial Rome. Etudes préliminaires aux religions orientales dans l'empire romain, 20 (Leiden, 1972), no. 302, p. 138 and pl. CCXV.

Cat. 40a-b: Brooklyn 52.1. Perhaps from Hierakonpolis. Height 54.5 cm.; width 19.0 cm.; depth 35.0 cm.; height of face 5.3 cm. Bibl.: Brooklyn 1952, no. 27, illus.; Brooklyn 1956, no. 3, pp. 3-4 and pls. 11-12; Vandier 1958, pp. 188-189 and pl. LXIII, 1; Brooklyn 1974a, no. 110, p. 48 and pl. XXXV; Brooklyn 1974b, pp. 38-39, illus.

Cat. 41: Brooklyn 39.602. Height 68.3 cm.; width 43.4 cm.; depth 48.9 cm., height of man's face 13.0 cm.; height of man's head 16.0 cm.; height of female figure 22.5 cm.; height of female figure's face 3.2 cm. Bibl.: Cooney, J. D., Journal of Egyptian Archaeology 35 (1949), pp. 153-157 and pl. XVII; Aldred, C., Middle Kingdom Art in Ancient Egypt (London, 1950), no. 75, pp. 53-54, illus.; Vandier 1958, pp. 236, 251, 254 and pl. LXXX, 6; Bothmer, B. V., The Brooklyn Museum Annual II-III, 1960-1962 (Brooklyn, 1963), no. V, p. 29 and fig. 10, p. 34; Brooklyn 1974a, no. 139, pp. 59-60 and pl. XL.

Cat. 42: Lowie 5-352. Height 59.5 cm.; width 43.5 cm.; depth 10.0 cm. Bibl.: California 1927, no. 77, pp. 7, 21 and pl. 39; California 1966, p. 63, illus.

Cat. 43: Lowie 6-13336. Naga ed-Deir, Cemetery 100, Tomb 361. Height 6.4 cm.; width 3.2 cm. Bibl.: none. Cf. Wilkinson, A., Ancient Egyptian Jewellery (London, 1971), p. 61, fig. 39.

Cat. 44: Lowie 6-22881. Naga ed-Deir, Cemetery 1500, Tomb 76. Height 2.2 cm.; width 1.8 cm. Bibl.: California 1966, p. 58, illus.

Cat. 45: Brooklyn 44.226. Height 13.1 cm.; width 5.1 cm.; depth 2.6 cm.; height of face 2.0 cm. Bibl.: Brooklyn 1968, no. 5, p. 11, illus. and p. 93.

Cat. 46: Lowie 6-19513. Qena. Height 14.5 cm. Bibl.: California 1966, p. 70, illus.

Cat. 47: Lowie 6-17311. Deir el Ballas. Length 23.3 cm. Bibl.: California 1966, p. 67, illus.; California 1968, p. 82, illus.

Cat. 48: Brooklyn 71.82. Karnak. Height 31.1 cm.; width 19.5 cm.; depth 3.0 cm.; height of face 9.6 cm. Bibl.: The Brooklyn Museum Annual XIII, 1971-1972 (Brooklyn 1973), p. 8. This relief will be published by B. V. Bothmer in a study of the reliefs of Amenhotep I (in preparation).

Cat. 49: Brooklyn 61.196. Height 38.1 cm.; width 13.4 cm.; depth 19.0 cm.; height of face 4.6 cm. Bibl.: Bothmer, B. V., The Brooklyn Museum Annual VIII, 1966-1967 (Brooklyn, 1968), pp. 55-61, figs. 1-4; Sauneron, S., Kêmi 18 (1968), pp. 45-50, pls. V-VII; Brooklyn 1974a, no. 178, pp. 77-78 and pl. XLVII.

Cat. 50a-b: Brooklyn 37.249E. Probably from Thebes. Height 23.3 cm.; width 11.5 cm.; depth 15.7 cm.; height of face 4.4 cm. Bibl.: Vandier 1958, p. 452; Brooklyn 1974a, no. 208, p. 90 and pl. LIII.

Cat. 51: Lowie 6-8436. Deir el Ballas. Length 18.2 cm.; width 4.0 cm. Bibl.: California 1966, p. 68, illus.; California 1968, p. 82, illus.

Cat. 52: Brooklyn 40.298. Height 9.2 cm.; diameter of rim 26.3 cm. *Bibl.:* Brooklyn 1968, no. 14, p. 18, illus., p. 95 and pl. III; Strauss, E-C., *Die Nunschale. Eine Gefässgruppe des Neuen Reiches.* Münchner Aegyptologische Studien, 30 (Munich, 1974), p. 16.

Cat. 53: Lowie 6-15174. Naga ed-Deir, Cemetery 9000. Length 38.0 cm.; width 5.2 cm. *Bibl.:* none.

Cat. 54a-b: Brooklyn 67.68. Armant. Height 47.2 cm.; width 17.5 cm.; depth 29.3 cm.; height of face 5.4 cm. *Bibl.:* Bothmer, B. V., *The Brooklyn Museum Annual VIII, 1966-1967* (Brooklyn, 1968), pp. 61-63, figs. 5-8; Bothmer, B. V., *The Brooklyn Museum Annual XI, 1969-1970,* pt. 2 (Brooklyn, 1971), pp. 125-143, fig. 1; Brooklyn 1974a, no. 177, pp. 75-77 and pl. XLVI; Brooklyn 1974b, pp. 44-45, illus.

Cat. 55: Brooklyn 56.7. Height 31.1 cm.; width 24.0 cm.; height of face 15.7 cm. *Bibl.:* Brooklyn 1956, no. 7, p. 6 and pls. 16-17; Vandier 1958, p. 306.

Cat. 56: Lowie 5-365. Probably from the Temple of Mut at Karnak. Height 74.3 cm.; width 42.0 cm.; depth 42.0 cm. *Bibl.:* California 1930, no. 1 and pl. 1a; California 1966, p. 74, illus.

Cat. 57a: Brooklyn 65.197. Thebes, Tomb 181. Height of figure 30.2 cm. *Bibl.:* Schott, S., *Das schöne Fest vom Wüstentale. Festbräuche einer Totenstadt* (Wiesbaden, 1952), no. 43, p. 106; Brooklyn 1974a, no. 252e, p. 112 and pl. LXXXIX; Brooklyn 1974b, pp. 48-49, illus.

Cat. 57b: Photograph of Theban Tomb No. 181. Photography by The Egyptian Expedition, The Metropolitan Museum of Art.

Cat. 58: Brooklyn 59.2. Height 29.6 cm.; diameter of rim 12.4 cm.; diameter of body 16.0 cm. *Bibl.:* Aldred, C., *Akhenaten, Pharaoh of Egypt; A New Study* (London, 1968), pp. 118-119, fig. 35, p. 156 and pl. X.

Cat. 59: Brooklyn 58.28.8. Height 5.3 cm.; width 5.6 cm.; depth 5.0 cm. *Bibl.:* Brooklyn 1968, no. 25, p. 26, illus., p. 97 and pl. II.

Cat. 60: Brooklyn 47.120.3. Kom Medinet Ghurab. Height 15.6 cm.; width 4.2 cm.; depth 3.4 cm.; height of face 2.0 cm.; width of base 3.5 cm.; depth of base 5.5 cm. *Bibl.:* Brooklyn 1952, no. 33, illus.; Vandier 1958, pp. 438, 491, 501, 525 and pl. CLXXIII, 4; Brooklyn 1974a, no. 284, p. 126 and pls. XI, LXXIII.

Cat. 61: Brooklyn 69.45. Probably from Thebes. Height 56.0 cm.; width 28.8 cm.; depth 24.4 cm.; height of face 9.3 cm. *Bibl.:* Aldred, C., *Journal of Egyptian Archaeology* 45 (1959), p. 23; Brooklyn 1974a, no. 287, pp. 127-128 and pl. LXXIV.

Cat. 62: Brooklyn 64.199.2. Karnak. Height 17.0 cm.; width 29.5 cm.; depth 3.0 cm. *Bibl.:* The Brooklyn Museum Annual VI, 1964-1965 (Brooklyn, 1966), p. 17, illus.

Cat. 63: Brooklyn 16.48. Tell el Amarna. Height 15.7 cm.; width 22.1 cm.; depth 4.2 cm. *Bibl.:* Aldred 1973, no. 121, pp. 190-191, illus.; Brooklyn 1974b, pp. 52-53, illus.

Cat. 64: Brooklyn 29.34. Tell el Amarna, House Q. 44.4. Height 21.9 cm.; width 4.8 cm.; depth 4.4 cm.; height of face 2.3 cm. *Bibl.:* Brooklyn 1952, no. 34, illus.; Vandier 1958, pp. 336-338, 348-349 and pl. CX, 4; Aldred 1973, no. 96, p. 168, illus.

Cat. 65: Brooklyn 33.52. Tell el Amarna, the Royal Tomb. Height 6.4 cm.; width 8.2 cm.; depth 7.6 cm.; height of face, 4.0 cm. *Bibl.:* Aldred 1973, no. 161, p. 217, illus.

Cat. 66a-b: Brooklyn 60.197.6. Tell el Amarna; found at Hermopolis. Height 23.1 cm.; width 51.5 cm.; depth 3.9 cm.; height of face 5.2 cm. *Bibl.:* Cooney 1965, no. 4, pp. 9-11, illus.; Roeder 1969, no. P.C. 24, p. 404 and pl. 173; Aldred 1973, no. 116, p. 185, illus.

Cat. 67: Brooklyn 62.149. Tell el Amarna; found at Hermopolis. Height 22.0 cm.; width 54.3 cm.; depth 3.7 cm. *Bibl.:* Cooney 1965, no. 46, pp. 73-74, illus.; Roeder 1969, no. P.C. 84, p. 406 and pl. 184; Aldred 1973, no. 69, p. 144, illus.

Cat. 68: Brooklyn 60.197.5. Tell el Amarna; found at Hermopolis. Height 23.1 cm.; width 52.5 cm.; depth 3.4 cm. *Bibl.:* Cooney 1965, no. 37, pp. 60-61, illus.; Roeder 1969, no. P.C. 40, p. 405 and pl. 174; Aldred 1973, no. 144, p. 207, illus.

Cat. 69: Brooklyn 60.197.8. Tell el Amarna; found at Hermopolis. Height 23.2 cm.; width 45.2 cm.; depth 3.4 cm.; height of queen's face 10.0 cm.; height of head of princess 6.4 cm. *Bibl.:* Cooney 1965, no. 12, pp. 20-22, illus.; Roeder 1969, no. P.C. 28, p. 404 and pl. 172; Aldred 1973, no. 92, pp. 164-165, illus.

Cat. 70: Brooklyn 47.120.1. Memphis. Height 14.4 cm.; width 31.3 cm.; depth 3.0 cm.; height of face 4.6 cm. *Bibl.:* Riefstahl, E., *Journal of Near Eastern Studies* 10 (1951), pp. 65-73, pls. I-II; Smith, W. S., *The Art and Architecture of Ancient Egypt* (Baltimore, 1958), p. 209 and pl. 145b; Aldred, C., *New Kingdom Art in Ancient Egypt,* 2nd ed., rev. (London, 1961), no. 111, pp. 74-75, illus.

Cat. 71: Brooklyn 66.174.1. Sumenu. Height 47.2 cm.; width 25.1 cm.; depth 31.0 cm.; height of face 8.3 cm. *Bibl.:* Bothmer, B. V., *The Brooklyn Museum Annual VIII, 1966-1967* (Brooklyn, 1968), pp. 84-89, figs. 30-34; Sauneron, S., *Kêmi* 18 (1968), pp. 66-78, pls. XII-XIII.

Cat. 72: Brooklyn 60.27.1. Height 22.2 cm.; diameter of disk 12.2 cm. *Bibl.:* The Brooklyn Museum Annual I, 1959-1960 (Brooklyn, 1962), p. 40, illus.

Cat. 73: Brooklyn 40.522. Thebes. Width 36.6 cm.; depth 11.3 cm. *Bibl.:* Brooklyn 1968, no. 32, p. 31, illus., p. 99 and pl. IX.

Cat. 74: Brooklyn 48.181. Said to be from Tell el Amarna. Height 5.4 cm.; width of base 4.0 cm.; depth of base 2.9 cm.; height of monkey 5.0 cm.; width of monkey 2.8 cm.; depth of monkey 4.2 cm. *Bibl.:* Aldred, C., *New Kingdom Art in Ancient Egypt,* 2nd ed., rev. (London, 1961), no. 77, pp. 64-65, illus.; Brooklyn 1968, no. 26, p. 27, illus., pp. 97-98 and pl. II.

Cat. 75: Brooklyn 37.605E. Saqqara. Length 29.5 cm.; width 8.3 cm. *Bibl.:* Riefstahl, E., *Toilet Articles from Ancient Egypt* (Brooklyn, 1943), no. 16, illus.; Wallert, I., *Der verzierte Löffel . . . .* Aegyptologische Abhandlungen, 16 (Wiesbaden, 1967), no. B 49, p. 83 and pl. 28.

Cat. 76: Brooklyn 37.413. Sesebi. Height 39.4 cm.; width 56.0 cm.; depth 18.0 cm. *Bibl.:* Riefstahl, E., *The Brooklyn Museum Bulletin 17, no. 4* (Summer, 1956), pp. 2-6, fig. 1.

Cat. 77: Brooklyn 11.670. Abydos, temple of Ramesses II. Height 42.5 cm.; width 38.5 cm.; depth 9.0 cm.; height of face 12.4 cm. *Bibl.:* Cooney, J. D., *Bulletin of the Cleveland Museum of Art 54* (1969), p. 288, illus.; Fazzini, R., *Miscellanea Wilbouriana 1* (Brooklyn, 1972), pp. 50-51, fig. 18.

Cat. 78: Brooklyn 61.20. Height of sphinx 12.8 cm.; length 12.5 cm.; width 4.2 cm.; height of face 1.3 cm. *Bibl.:* The Brooklyn Museum Annual II-III, 1960-1962 (Brooklyn, 1963), p. 71, illus. and p. 73; Houston, Texas, Art Department of the University of St. Thomas. *Constant Companions. An Exhibition of Mythological Animals . . . October 28, 1964-February 7, 1965* (Houston, 1964), no. 1, p. 3, illus.

Cat. 79: Brooklyn 48.30.2a-b. Saqqara. Height 45.9 cm.; height of jar 35.0 cm.; diameter of jar 18.0 cm.; height of lid 13.4 cm.; height of face 6.9 cm. *Bibl.* Brooklyn 1952, no. 49, illus.

Cat. 80: Brooklyn 36.261. Saqqara. Height 52.0 cm.; width 44.5 cm.; height of face 10.6 cm. *Bibl.:* Schaefer, H., and Andrae, W., *Die Kunst des alten Orients.* Propyläen-Kunstgeschichte, II, 3rd ed. (Berlin, 1942), p. 683 and pl. 396, 2; Brooklyn 1974b, pp. 54-55, illus.

Cat. 81: Brooklyn 68.150.1. Height 30.8 cm.; width 56.0 cm.; depth 6.5 cm. *Bibl.: The Brooklyn Museum Annual X, 1968-1969* (Brooklyn, 1969), p. 167.

Cat. 82: Lowie 6-22249. Found or purchased at El Ahaiwah in June of 1900. Length 18.5 cm.; width 8.6 cm. *Bibl.: California 1966*, p. 69, illus.

Cat. 83: Lowie 6-15558. Naga ed-Deir. Height 20.0 cm.; width 21.0 cm. *Bibl.:* none.

Cat. 84: Brooklyn 37.51E. Thebes. Height 8.9 cm.; width 16.9 cm.; depth 0.6-1.1 cm. *Bibl.:* Riefstahl, E., *The Brooklyn Museum Bulletin* 13, no. 2 (Winter, 1952), p. 5, fig. 3; Brunner-Traut, E., *Altaegyptische Tiergeschichte und Fabel; Gestalt und Strahlkraft,* 2nd ed., (Darmstadt, 1968), pp. 7-8, 2. Belege a and p. 68.

Cat. 85: Brooklyn 36.835. Height 11.3 cm.; width 7.5 cm.; depth 10.3 cm.; height of face 5.6 cm. *Bibl.:* London, Sotheby & Co. *Catalogue of the Amherst Collection of Egyptian Antiquities . . . Monday, the 13th of June, 1921 . . .* (London, 1921), p. 27, lot 258 and pl. VIII. The author would like to thank Mr. John D. Cooney for providing him with a copy of the manuscript for an article in which Mr. Cooney will publish this head in more detail.

Cat. 86: Brooklyn 58.92. Height 2.4 cm.; width 2.4 cm. *Bibl.:* Brooklyn 1974b, pp. 60-61, illus.; Cooney, J. D., *Bulletin of the Cleveland Museum of Art* 62 (1975), pp. 15-16, fig. 7.

Cat. 87: Brooklyn 37.254E. Memphis. Height 20.2 cm.; width 3.7 cm.; depth 3.7 cm.; height of face 1.2 cm. *Bibl.:* Williams, C. R., *New-York Historical Society Quarterly Bulletin* 3 (1919), pp. 71-72, fig. 1; Roeder, G., *Aegyptische Bronzefiguren.* Staatliche Museen zu Berlin. Mitteilungen aus der aegyptischen Sammlung, VI (Berlin, 1956), p. 34, para. 57, a.

Cat. 88: Brooklyn 67.118. Mendes. Height 52.3 cm.; width 32.3 cm.; depth 6.5 cm. *Bibl.:* Kitchen, K. A., *Journal of the American Research Center in Egypt* 8 (1969-1970), pp. 59-67, figs. 1-3.

Cat. 89: Brooklyn 59.17. Height 29.3 cm.; width 15.9 cm. *Bibl.:* Brooklyn 1968, no. 59, p. 61, illus. and p. 106; Kitchen, K. A., *The Third Intermediate Period in Egypt (1100-650 B.C.),* (Warminster, 1973) pp. 124-125, 341-342, 360; Gomaà, F., *Die libyschen Fürstentümer des Deltas . . . .* Beihefte zum Tübinger Atlas des vorderen Orients Reihe B (Geisteswissenschaften), Nr. 5 (Wiesbaden, 1974), pp. 120-121.

Cat. 90: Brooklyn 60.74. Height 7.1 cm.; width 5.3 cm.; depth 6.5 cm.; height of face 3.9 cm. *Bibl.:* Russmann, E., *The Brooklyn Museum Annual X, 1968-1969* (Brooklyn, 1969), pp. 97-101, figs. 10-12; Russmann, E., *The Representation of the King in the XXVth Dynasty.* Monographies Reine Elisabeth, 3. (Brussels and Brooklyn, 1974), no. 27, pp. 14-15, 52-53 and fig. 5.

Cat. 91: Brooklyn 54.198. Height 3.9 cm.; width 3.0 cm.; depth 1.7 cm. *Bibl.:* Brooklyn 1956, no. 68, p. 55 and pl. 86; Russmann, E., *The Representation of the King in the XXVth Dynasty.* Monographies Reine Elisabeth, 3. (Brussels and Brooklyn, 1974), p. 26.

Cat. 92: Brooklyn 39.2. Nuri, Pyramid 1. Height 40.2 cm.; width 13.7 cm.; depth 8.5 cm. *Bibl.:* none.

Cat. 93a-b: Brooklyn 64.149. Height 11.0 cm.; width 10.0 cm.; depth 6.3 cm. *Bibl.: The Brooklyn Museum Annual VI, 1964-1965* (Brooklyn, 1966), p. 64.

Cat. 94: Brooklyn 64.146. Tell el Moqdam. Height 46.3 cm.; width 22.0 cm.; depth 31.2 cm.; height of face 7.2 cm. *Bibl.:* Bothmer, B. V., *Kêmi* 20 (1970), pp. 37-48, pls. VI-VII.

Cat. 95: Lowie 5-363. Thebes, Tomb 34. Height 51.0 cm.; width 35.7 cm.; depth 28.5 cm. *Bibl.:* California 1930, no. 1b, p. 1 and pl. 1b; Bothmer, B. V., et al, *Egyptian Sculpture of the Late Period. 700 B.C. to A.D. 100* (Brooklyn, 1960), no. 17, p. 19 and pl. 15; Leclant, J., *Drevni Mir, Mélanges V. V. Struve* (Moscow, 1962), no. IV, pp. 121-122, fig. 23.

Cat. 96a: Brooklyn 48.74. Thebes, Tomb 34. Height 23.9 cm.; width 28.7 cm. *Bibl.:* Cooney, J. D., *Journal of Near Eastern Studies* 9 (1950), pp. 193-197, pl. XIV; Smith, W. S., *The Art and Architecture of Ancient Egypt* (Baltimore, 1958), pp. 247-248 and pl. 180; Leclant, J., *Montouemhat, quatrième prophète d'Amon . . . .* Institut Français d'Archéologie Orientale, Bibliothèque d'Etude, XXXV (Cairo, 1961), p. 183.

Cat. 96b-c: Paintings in Tomb 69 at Thebes. After Cooney, J. D., *Journal of Near Eastern Studies* 9 (1950), pl. XV.

Cat. 97a: Brooklyn 52.131.3. Thebes, Tomb 312. Height 34.5 cm.; width 55.5 cm.; depth 8.5 cm. *Bibl.:* Winlock, H. E., *Excavations at Deir el Bahri, 1911-1931* (New York, 1942), pp. 81-83 and pl. 91; Brooklyn 1956, no. 35 C, pp. 32-33 and pl. 59. E. Russmann, who is preparing a study of the tomb of Nespekashuty, has contributed valuable comments on this relief.

Cat. 97b: Brooklyn 52.131.24-.25. The relief from the tomb of Mentuemhat in The Fine Arts Museums of San Francisco has been published by B. Lesko in *Journal of the American Research Center in Egypt* 9 (1971-1972), pp. 85-88, fig. 1.

Cat. 98a-b: Brooklyn 71.11. Height of figure 13.6 cm.; width 5.7 cm.; depth 7.0 cm.; height of face 2.2 cm. *Bibl.:* New York, Parke-Bernet Galleries, Inc. *The Notable Art Collection [of] Mr. Joseph Brummer . . . May 11, 1949* (New York, 1949), p. 5, lot 22, illus.; *The Brooklyn Museum Annual XII, 1970-1971* (Brooklyn, 1971), p. 21.

Cat. 99: Brooklyn 05.394. Height 28.8 cm.; width 9.5 cm.; depth 21.4 cm. *Bibl.:* Pritchard, J. B., *The Ancient Near East in Pictures Relating to the Old Testament* (Princeton, 1954), p. 189; fig. 564 and pp. 317-318.

Cat. 100: Brooklyn 07.422. Thebes. Height 50.8 cm.; width 36.2 cm.; depth 14.3 cm. *Bibl.:* none.

Cat. 101: Lowie 6-19880. Akhmim. Height 75.5 cm.; width 48.7 cm.; depth 11.0 cm. *Bibl.:* California 1930, no. 86, pl. 44; De Meulenaere, H., *Mitteilungen des Deutschen Archäologischen Instituts. Abteilung Kairo* 25 (1969), p. 91; California 1966, p. 78, illus.; Westendorff, W., *Altaegyptische Darstellungen des Sonnenlaufs . . . .* Münchner Aegyptologische Studien, 10 (Berlin, 1966), pp. 88-89 and pl. 38; Munro, P., *Lexikon der Aegyptologie,* Vol. I, pt. 4 (Wiesbaden, 1973), col. 585; Munro, P., *Die spätägyptischen Totenstelen.* Aegyptologische Forschungen, 25 (Glückstadt, 1973), p. 313.

Cat. 102. Lowie 6-19929. Possibly from Tebtunis. Length 173.0 cm. *Bibl.:* none.

Cat. 103a-b: Brooklyn 52.89. Probably from the Delta. Height 51.2 cm.; width 16.7 cm.; depth 14.0 cm.; height of face 5.4 cm. *Bibl.:* Brooklyn 1956, no. 14, pp. 14-15 and pls. 30-31; Bothmer, B. V., et al, *Egyptian Sculpture of the Late Period. 700 B.C. to A.D. 100* (Brooklyn, 1960), no. 80, pp. 100-101 and pl. 76.

Cat. 104a-b.: Brooklyn 55.175. Karnak, Cachette. Height 15.3 cm.; width 10.0 cm.; depth 12.7 cm. *Bibl.:* Bothmer, B. V., et al, *Egyptian Sculpture of the Late Period. 700 B.C. to A.D. 100* (Brooklyn, 1960), no. 83, pp. 105-106 and pl. 79; Bothmer, B. V., *The Brooklyn Museum Annual IV, 1962-1963* (Brooklyn, 1963), pp. 42-51, illus.; Brooklyn 1974b, pp. 76-77, illus.

Cat. 104c: Brooklyn 55.175 with its body: Cairo, Egyptian Museum J. E. 38064.

Cat. 105: Brooklyn 37.37E. Benha el Assel. Height 45.0 cm.; width 34.5 cm.; depth 20.5 cm.; height of face 15.7 cm. *Bibl.*: Bothmer, B. V., et al, *Egyptian Sculpture of the Late Period. 700 B.C. to A.D. 100* (Brooklyn, 1960), p. 122.

Cat. 106: Brooklyn 72.127. Probably from Behbeit el Higara. Height 69.0 cm.; width 60.0 cm.; depth 6.0 cm. *Bibl.*: Steindorff, G., *Journal of the Walters Art Gallery VII-VIII, 1944-1945* (Baltimore, 1945), no. 18, p. 56, fig. 20.

Cat. 107: Brooklyn 37.1525E. Nubia. Height 48.5 cm.; width 69.0 cm.; depth 5.3 cm. *Bibl.*: Porter, B. and Moss, R., *Topographical Bibliography of Ancient Egyptian Hieroglyphic Texts, Reliefs, and Paintings. Vol. 7, Nubia, the Deserts, and Outside Egypt* (Oxford, 1951), p. 273.

Cat. 108a-b.: Brooklyn 69.115.1. Thebes. Height 39.0 cm.; width 16.7 cm.; depth 20.0 cm.; height of face 6.2 cm. *Bibl.: The Brooklyn Museum Annual XI, 1969-1970,* pt. 1 (Brooklyn, 1971), pp. 22-23, illus.; Fischer, H. G., *Zeitschrift für ägyptische Sprache* 100 (1973), p. 27.

Cat. 109: Brooklyn 71.37.2. Thebes. Height 37.5 cm.; width 27.0 cm.; depth 4.2 cm. *Bibl.: The Brooklyn Museum Annual* XII, 1970-1971 (Brooklyn, 1971), p. 21. This stela and other monuments belonging to members of the same family are being studied by H. De Meulenaere, who has kindly provided information about this stela.

Cat. 110: Brooklyn 37.804E. Saqqara. Height 3.1 cm.; width 6.8 cm.; depth 0.5 cm. *Bibl.*: Williams, C. R., *Gold and Silver Jewelry and Related Objects. The New York Historical Society. Catalogue of Ancient Egyptian Antiquities. Numbers 1-160* (New York, 1924), no. 104, pp. 172-174 and pls. XXVIIa,b, XXIX,c; Aldred, C., *Jewels of the Pharaohs. Egyptian Jewellery of the Dynastic Period* (London, 1971), pp. 241-242 and pls. 142-143.

Cat. 111: Brooklyn 49.28. Width (total) 25.5 cm.; height of scarab 2.1 cm.; length of scarab 6.3 cm.; width of scarab 4.2 cm.; length of wings 9.6 cm.; width of wings 3.5 cm.; depth of wings 0.5 cm. *Bibl.*: Brooklyn 1968, no. 66, p. 68, illus. and p. 108.

Cat. 112: Brooklyn 65.3.2. Height 3.0 cm.; width 4.0 cm. *Bibl.*: Brooklyn 1968, no. 74, p. 75, illus., pp. 109-110 and pl. XI.

Cat. 113a-b: Brooklyn 64.198. Height 10.6 cm.; width 5.2 cm.; depth 3.4 cm. *Bibl.*: Brooklyn 1968, no. 72, p. 72, illus. and p. 109.

Cat. 114: Brooklyn 60.73. Height 23.2 cm.; width 13.5 cm.; depth 5.8 cm. *Bibl.*: Jacquet-Gordon, H., *The Brooklyn Museum Annual VII, 1965-1966* (Brooklyn, 1966), pp. 53-64, figs. 1, 2, 5, 6.

Cat. 115: Brooklyn 57.42. Mitrahineh (Memphis). Height 14.7 cm.; width 6.0 cm.; depth 12.0 cm. *Bibl.*: Bothmer, B. V., et al, *Egyptian Sculpture of the Late Period. 700 B.C. to A.D. 100* (Brooklyn, 1960), no. 106, p. 136 and pl. 98.

Cat. 116a-b: Lowie 8-4586. Height 31.8 cm.; width 19.8 cm.; depth 25.5 cm. *Bibl.*: Cheney, S., *Sculpture of the World; A History* (New York, 1968), p. 56, illus.

Cat. 117a-b: Brooklyn 58.30. Mitrahineh (Memphis). Height 41.4 cm.; width 28.5 cm.; depth 34.0 cm. *Bibl.*: Bothmer, B. V., et al, *Egyptian Sculpture of the Late Period. 700 B.C. to A.D. 100* (Brooklyn, 1960), no. 132, pp. 172-173 and pls. 123-124; Brooklyn 1974b, pp. 90-91, illus.

Note

The following measurements correct and augment data given in catalogue entries and in Concordance I

Cat. 3: height 25.2 cm.; width 14.0 cm.; diameter of rim 8.6 cm.
Cat. 4: height 8.0 cm.; width 15.6 cm.; width of base 5.6 cm.
Cat. 5: height 13.5 cm.; greatest diameter 17.5 cm.; diameter of rim 11.0 cm.
Cat. 6: height 21.8 cm.; diameter of rim 12.0 cm.
Cat. 7: length 18.8 cm.; width 7.3 cm.
Cat. 9: length 9.0 cm.; width 5.9 cm.
Cat. 10: height 17.8 cm.; length 39.0 cm.; thickness 4.0 cm.
Cat. 13: height 4.9 cm.; greatest diameter 20.2 cm.
Cat. 14: length 28.0 cm.
Cat. 17: height 44.7 cm.; width 67.5 cm.
Cat. 21: height 37.0 cm.; width across shoulders 12.0 cm.; height of face 5.0 cm.; height of base 3.5 cm.; width of base 12.0 cm.; depth of base 21.0 cm.; width of back pillar 3.5 cm.
Cat. 22: height 40.5 cm.; height of figure 37.5 cm.; width across shoulders 9.9 cm.; height of face 4.3 cm.; width of base 10.5 cm.; depth of base 17.0 cm.; width of back pillar 9.2 cm.

Cat. 23: height 43.5 cm.; width across man's shoulders 14.5 cm.; width across woman's shoulders 11.0 cm.; height of man's face 5.3 cm.; height of woman's face 4.6 cm.; height of base 4.0 cm.; width of base 26.0 cm.; depth of base 26.0 cm.; width of back slab 19.3 cm.
Cat. 24: height 72.0 cm.; height of figures 64.0 cm.; width across man's shoulders 20.0 cm.; width across woman's shoulders 17.0 cm.; height of man's face 6.7 cm.; height of woman's face 5.9 cm.; height of base 8.0 cm.; width of base 33.0 cm.; depth of base 25.5 cm.
Cat. 26: height 45.7 cm.; width 14.7 cm.; height of face 7.0 cm.
Cat. 27: height 18.0 cm.; width 12.0 cm.; depth 35.0 cm.; height of figure 15.5 cm.; width of figure 8.0 cm.; height of face 4.4 cm.; height of base 2.5 cm.
Cat. 28: height 40.2 cm.; height of figure 36.3 cm.; width across shoulders 7.8 cm.; height of face 4.2 cm.; height of base 3.9 cm.; width of base 7.4 cm.; depth of base 15.0 cm.
Cat. 34: height 75.6 cm.; width 100.0 cm.
Cat. 43: height 5.8 cm.; width 3.0 cm.
Cat. 44: height 1.8 cm.; width 1.5 cm.
Cat. 46: height 15.2 cm.; width 4.3 cm.; depth 3.7 cm.
Cat. 51: length 18.5 cm.; depth 1.3 cm.
Cat. 53: depth 0.96 cm.
Cat. 56: height 75.4 cm.; width 42.5 cm.; depth 49.0 cm.: height of face 24.7 cm.
Cat. 82: length 18.7 cm.; thickness 0.70 cm.
Cat. 83: height 21.0 cm.; depth 2.0-2.6 cm.
Cat. 95: height 50.0 cm.; width 35.0 cm.; depth 28.0 cm.; height of Imsety 34.0 cm.; width of Imsety 9.8 cm.; height of Hapy 35.0 cm.; width of Hapy 9.8 cm.; height of Imsety's face 5.0 cm.; height of Hapy's face 3.0 cm.; height of base 15.0 cm.
Cat. 102: length 171.0 cm.; width 41.5 cm.; depth 28.5 cm.

Concordance II

Accession numbers: Catalogue numbers

Berkeley, Robert H. Lowie Museum of Anthropology

Acc. No.	Cat. No.	Acc. No.	Cat. No.	Acc. No.	Cat. No.
5-352	42	6-16024	29	6-19784	13
5-363	95	6-17171	9	6-19825	17
5-365	56	6-17311	47	6-19870	34
6-1903	30	6-17557	7	6-19880	101
6-3329	5	6-17633	3	6-19881	31
6-3586	2	6-19071	10	6-19929	102
6-4015	6	6-19513	46	6-22233	8
6-4735	4	6-19760	23	6-22249	82
6-8436	51	6-19766	27	6-22881	44
6-13336	43	6-19768	26	6-22883	14
6-15174	53	6-19770	21	8-4586	116
6-15215	28	6-19772	22		
6-15558	83	6-19775	24		

Brooklyn, The Brooklyn Museum

Acc. No.	Cat. No.	Acc. No.	Cat. No.	Acc. No.	Cat. No.
05.394	99	47.120.3	60	60.197.6	66
07.422	100	48.30.2a-b	79	60.197.8	69
07.447.502	1	48.74	96a	61.20	78
11.670	77	48.181	74	61.196	49
16.48	63	49.28	111	62.149	67
29.34	64	51.231	32	64.146	94
33.52	65	52.1	40	64.149	93
36.261	80	52.89	103	64.198	113
36.835	85	52.129	36a	64.199.2	62
37.413	76	52.130.2	37	65.3.2	112
37.16E	35	52.131.3	97a	65.197	57a
37.17E	25	54.49	33a	66.174.1	71
37.25E	20a	54.198	91	67.68	54
37.37E	105	55.175	104	67.118	88
37.51E	84	56.7	55	68.150.1	81
37.249E	50	56.85	39	68.152	16
37.254E	87	57.42	115	69.45	61
37.605E	75	58.28.8	59	69.115.1	108
37.804E	110	58.30	117	71.11	98
37.1525E	107	58.92	86	71.37.2	109
39.2	92	58.192	12	71.82	48
39.119	19	59.1	38	72.58	18
39.602	41	59.2	58	72.127	106
40.298	52	59.17	89	73.26	11
40.522	73	60.27.1	72		
44.226	45	60.73	114		
46.167	15	60.74	90		
47.120.1	70	60.197.5	68		